Leadersights

Creating Great Leaders Who Create Great Workplaces

Leadersights

Creating Great Leaders Who Create Great Workplaces

David Veech

CRC Press
Taylor & Francis Group
Boca Raton   London   New York

CRC Press is an imprint of the
Taylor & Francis Group, an **informa** business

A PRODUCTIVITY PRESS BOOK

CRC Press
Taylor & Francis Group
6000 Broken Sound Parkway NW, Suite 300
Boca Raton, FL 33487-2742

International Standard Book Number-13: 978-1-4665-5800-7 (Hardback)

Library of Congress Cataloging-in-Publication Data

Names: Veech, David, author.
Title: Leadersights : creating great leaders who create great workplaces / David Veech.
Description: Boca Raton, FL : CRC Press, [2017]
Identifiers: LCCN 2016033575 | ISBN 9781466558007 (hardback : alk. paper)
Subjects: LCSH: Leadership. | Self-efficacy. | Work environment.
Classification: LCC HD57.7 .V44 2017 | DDC 658.4/092--dc23
LC record available at https://lccn.loc.gov/2016033575

Visit the Taylor & Francis Web site at
http://www.taylorandfrancis.com

and the CRC Press Web site at
http://www.crcpress.com

To my surrogate grandmother Virginia Mason and my aunt Valerie Veech.

Virginia Mason, or Oma as we called her, was a woman of many accomplishments, from delivering babies in the Appalachian Mountains, to playing basketball on one of the first University of Louisville women's teams, to serving as an army nurse in World War II. She lived quietly and privately, but through her stories and service to her church she touched many lives.

Aunt Val was in many ways similar to Oma. She did many different things to support her family, even owning her own franchise at one point and working with the Sheriff's department. After my mother died, she invited us to spend Thanksgiving and Christmas with them, and every year she made my kids her grandkids and gave us all a place to call home.

When these wonderful women died, the outpouring of love at their funerals amazed me, and I could only think how both were true demonstrations of the power of servant leadership. I miss them every day.

Contents

Acknowledgments

I've spent more than 7 years as a principal at the Institute for Lean Systems (ILS), a firm dedicated to making organizations more competitive through implementing the principles of lean systems. During this time, my partners Parthi Damodaraswamy, Ray Littlefield, and Jon Yingling, challenged me to develop more practical applications for many of the topics I address in this book. In particular, their insights have contributed significantly to the chapters on visual management systems and standardized work.

As an assignment for one of my early psychology courses, I interviewed psychologist Tom Bergandi at Spaulding University in Louisville, who recommended I read Ken Wilbur's *Integral Psychology*. Reading Wilbur's book was pretty much like putting my brain in a blender; it fundamentally changed the way I think about organizations and leadership and has influenced the way I've worked ever since.

I originally met my former colleague Joachim Knuf as a teacher. Joachim has a different way of thinking about many things in lean systems, and he and I spent hours talking about leadership and change. His questioning of ideas most people look upon as "just common sense" reshaped the way I viewed the basic tools we taught in lean and brought home the influence that small things can have on the operating philosophy of an organization.

Arlie Hall, another former colleague, was teaching problem solving at Toyota one day when a proverbial "light bulb" went on for me. All of a sudden I was able to connect about a hundred separate dots related to lean. Once those dots connected, I could see the image of the workplace I've ever since been trying to teach people to create.

This book has taken much longer to write than I expected, largely because of my tendency to become distracted and focus my energies elsewhere. I finally managed to get to the finish line after getting some help from Mike Valentino, who I engaged to bug me until I sent everything to him and to do the final edit. Honestly, this project may never have been completed without him.

Finally, I have to thank my long-suffering wife, Mary Veech, who has put up with my cussing, whining, bragging, cheering, moaning, crying, etc. about this book for way too long. I think she always believed I would finish it, but I sure challenged her thinking toward that sometimes.

Although I'm extremely grateful for the ideas of these and many other people, past and present, whom I've encountered over the years, this book offers few specific citations from existing research. Still, everything I present stands on the shoulders of giants such as psychologists Abraham Maslow (peak experience), Edward Deci and Richard Ryan (intrinsic motivation), Robert Sternberg (cognitive development), management professors David McGregor (Theory X & Theory Y), Teresa Amabile (creativity), Albert Bandura (self-efficacy), Jim Collins (good to great organizations), Mihalyi Csikszentmihalyi (psychological flow), and Peter Senge (organizational learning); philosophers such as Ken Wilbur and Emmanual Kant, and countless others who have written and shared their brilliance with the world.

Author

David Veech thinks that work should be fun, exciting, challenging, and interesting, but most of all, it should be meaningful. He knows that leaders make or break this kind of workplace. He spends his time and energy teaching.

Veech teaches in the business school at The Ohio State University. He also teaches and coaches client companies around the world and delivers keynote addresses and seminars on topics related to leadership, problem solving, suggestion systems, employee engagement, team building, and creating satisfying workplaces. He has founded two nonprofit organizations to teach what he has learned to help solve critical problems such as access to quality education and safe healthcare in impoverished communities.

Veech is the author of *The C4 Process: Four Vital Steps to Better Work* (2011, Business Innovation Press, an imprint of Integrated Media Corp) (www.thec4process.com).

Veech holds a Bachelor of Arts degree in international relations from Western Kentucky University, and a Master of Science degree in industrial management from Clemson University. He has completed significant doctoral work in general and educational psychology at the University of Kentucky and Capella University.

Readers may contact him through email at david.veech@leadersights. com, on Twitter at @davidveech, or on LinkedIn at http://www.linkedin. com/in/davidveech. Readers are also welcome to send text messages or voice messages at 614-427-3309.

Introduction

Leadership books remind me of those old Sears & Roebuck catalogs—at least a couple in every home. Like the catalogs, the practical value of most leadership books seems best experienced when they land in the outhouse.

There's a glut of leadership books out there because—just as those Sears customers of long ago needed the merchandise (or maybe just the paper?) in those catalogs—people today need ideas that will help them become more effective leaders. I'm not going to say, "This book is different." It doesn't matter. Just read on. Reading helps our thinking, and as long as we're thinking, we're making progress.

I've struggled with the title for this book for months. Implying that I understand greatness is a real stretch for me. I've been practicing, studying, reading about, observing, and discussing leadership for more than 30 years. I have worked for only a couple of leaders whom I considered great. They made me want to work. They made me want to make them look more successful. They made me a better leader through their example.

I have been part of a couple of great workplaces. These are places where people feel connected to each other; where everyone cares about the organization and wants to contribute to its success; where everyone is focused and engaged. In my careers, these leaders and these workplaces are extremely rare. I want to change that. Over those 30 or so years, the most important thing I've learned about leadership is that a great leader has only one job: developing people. This means if you want to be a great leader, you have to teach. If you want to create a great workplace, you have to teach. This premise applies even when "leadership" is not part of your job description or your official title. If you're the person others come to for a challenge, for encouragement, for feedback, and for support, then you're a leader, whether you want to be or not.

> ## A great leader has only one job: To develop people

LEADERSIGHTS

This isn't a history book, so you won't find endless profiles of great men and women or case studies of great workplaces. What you will find are practical ideas you should try if you want to be a better leader and lead others to be great leaders. I hope this provides some *insight for leaders*, to shape them for the future. It doesn't matter where you work now, what you're doing, or how long you've been doing it. The key concepts, techniques, principles, and practices you need to master fall into one or more of three categories I call *leadersights*:

- Learning
- Loving
- Letting go

As a leader, even though you're still responsible for getting results, posting numbers, producing, etc., your most important job is still to teach others. It's not the job of Human Resources to teach them, it is your job. And if you want to teach effectively, you have to *learn* continuously to know what and how to teach; you have to *love* your employees like you love your children; and you have to *let go* and let them work. Throughout this book, I'll offer some very practical tools to use and explain how they serve to achieve a degree of greatness in a leader or a workplace. You will notice that Chapters 1 through 5 have a sprinkling of these little sections called leadersights. These earlier chapters are foundational and often more theoretical, so I've tried to offer practical activities to illustrate and reinforce some of these concepts. Chapter 6 is the pivotal leadership chapter describing a new model for leadership for workplaces to consider. Chapters 7 through 9 are all practical and don't need specific action call-outs or require special sections as the earlier chapters do. I've also included thought-provoking challenges or ideas that should make you question your own behavior as a leader. After all, if you weren't willing to change, you probably wouldn't be reading this book. So keep reading, but begin with the mindset that everything you're doing now is wrong. That's probably not true, but approaching this material with such a mindset will help you learn more effectively. Your learning must become new behavior for leading.

> ## Believe that everything you're doing now is wrong

REDEFINING CHANGE TO BUILD NEW SKILLS

We're going to be spending a lot of time in this book discussing change as a leadership concept—change in competitive marketplaces, change within organizations, and changes in individual behavior. Often, workplaces treat changes as discrete events (e.g., kaizen event, rapid improvement event, and action workout) or the implementation of a significant project (e.g., enterprise resource planning (ERP) system, electronic medical records, and moving into a new building). All these have a defined start date and a planned end date. Instead of thinking of change as a discrete initiative or event, we need to view it as simply the way we work.

Think of the way our daily lives are changing. Not long ago, we might have begun the day with a cup of coffee and the morning paper. By the time we left for work, we'd have caught up on world, national, and local events of the day before. In the evening, we would watch the news on TV to see what happened while we were at work. Checking in twice a day was enough for most of us; we were content to wait for the evening news and the morning newspaper to fill us in on the latest happenings. Today, we get our news in real time. The Internet and social media provide information in a continuous stream from millions of sources, all over the world, directly to our phones, tablets, or personal computers. TV news has become nostalgic, and newspapers are gasping their last breaths as most of us now expect up-to-the minute information literally at our fingertips. Now consider how much this sea change has affected the way we work.

Change management is a well-defined field of study; untold numbers of books have been written about driving change within organizations. Many of the classics of management literature, by celebrated authors such as Kurt Lewin, Darryl Conner, and John Kotter, focus on a common theme: There's a beginning (where we "unfreeze" or break free from existing methods with some "burning platform"), a middle (where we introduce new methods for dramatic improvement), and an end (where we "refreeze"—lock in or "anchor" new methods, building new behavioral habits as a result). In short, Lewin, Conner, and Kotter describe discrete change events.

One look at a Twitter feed and we see immediately that change is not discrete—it is continuous. In today's world, there isn't time to unfreeze, change, and refreeze. Instead of a standard approach, in which any change would disrupt a pattern of stability, we find ourselves in the midst of a river of changing rules, beliefs, guidelines, standards, methods, ideas, products, technologies, competitors, economies, and politics. There is no longer a discernable pattern of stability, and if we are to survive this new reality, change has to become the way we work rather than the way we make the transition from one way of working to another. We may still need to unfreeze in order to make a change, but if we try to refreeze after the change we'll never keep pace with the constantly shifting global landscape. Tomorrow's leaders will need to be comfortable operating in this swirling sea of ambiguity and complexity, because the stability in this dynamic environment comes not from rules and regulations but from the leaders themselves.

> **Change has to become the way we work; not the way we make the transition from one way of working to another**

One of the reasons many people fight change is lack of clarity. "Why do we have to do something differently?" "Aren't we already successful?" "If it ain't broke, why fix it?" Successful leaders bring clarity, comfort, and confidence to apparent chaos by: (1) effectively challenging people to achieve higher levels of performance, (2) providing support in a variety of ways, (3) encouraging people to take one more step, and (4) correcting improper or poor performance with compassionate feedback. Successful leaders can do these things even in those cases when the leaders themselves can't see the reason for change any more clearly than anyone else. They work through the ambiguity, and simplify what they can to provide as much guidance to their people as possible.

> # Within the complex mess that defines today's typical workplace, the leader is completely helpless

Oddly enough, within the complex mess that defines today's typical workplace, the leader is completely helpless. Read that again, because unless you realize the leader is helpless—that *you* are helpless—any effort you make to gain control will only make things worse. As frightening as it sounds, letting go is the only way to successfully lead for the long haul. We're operating in an environment now that requires as much predictability as we can muster, with as much flexibility as we can imagine. For this "dynamic stability" in workplaces, we need some boundaries with handrails that keep us heading mostly in the right direction, giving us some predictability, but still leaving us completely free to respond to other things that demand our attention; giving us flexibility. The handrails, the rules, and structures we build into our workplaces, should give us a sense of stability—as if we can always reach out and grab them when we find ourselves slipping—while at the same time leaving the path unobstructed so we can do whatever is needed to respond to a new challenge or opportunity. For this book, these handrails will take the form of work structures such as standardized work, visual management systems, and defined problem-solving processes. These give us strict parameters within which to work but remain open and flexible enough to allow experimentation and adjustment to provide what our internal and external customers may need.

Back in 2001, I wrote a paper describing an organizational form I called the Amoeba Model. This paper was later revised and published in *Cost Management* (Veech, D. S. 2004b). The concept, which has since shown up in a few other places, describes an extremely flexible workplace that also provides the overall stability necessary to build skills and maintain momentum, rather than stall in entropy. Dee Hock, founder and former CEO of Visa International, has coined the term "chaordic" to describe the necessity of working on the boundary between chaos and order, and it is exactly this type of organization we want to create.

Chaordic workplaces can survive and thrive in volatile, unstructured, chaotic, and complex times like those that exist today in our global marketplace. I call these Vigorous Learning Organizations, or VLOs, which were first described by Robert Hall in his book *Compression: Meeting the Challenges of Sustainability through Vigorous Learning Enterprises*. To thrive in the future, where complex problems challenge the most gifted of leaders, I believe the VLO is the only solution. The VLO to me is "What's Next." I'll flesh out this concept of the VLO as we progress.

SLOP AND MAGIC

Navigating a changing environment is tough enough, but if we're going to compete in a cutthroat global marketplace, we have to do more than respond to change; we have to create change. It is getting harder to obtain resources. The environment is becoming more sensitive and fragile. Consumption is increasing in wealthy places, and in poorer places, people are pushing back on authority to say "Enough!"

For years, leaders have asked people to do more with less. In a lot of minds, lean thinking means everyone doing more with less (more work, less people). Unfortunately, it isn't enough for a workplace to simply continue trying to do more with less. We have to do *better* with less. And that requires substantial innovation.

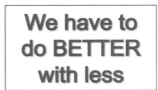

Innovation is the magic we need to create workplaces with the stability to succeed now, and the flexibility to succeed tomorrow. Innovation is the result of someone or some group challenging the way the rest of us think, the way we do things, and the things we do them with. It looks like magic to people with conventional thinking. Can we build that challenging mindset into our daily work, so that innovative behavior follows innovative thinking? Can we create magic?

People almost always behave and make decisions based on their experiences. There's nothing wrong with that. Doing something today the same way as yesterday provides a feeling of stability, and when people do the same thing again and again, they usually become better at it. What they don't become is innovative, because true innovation can't come from experience. To be innovative, we have to drive people beyond the limits of their experience, challenging and changing the way they think about products, service, processes, and customers; in fact, changing the way they think about everything. That means we, as leaders have to change the way we think about leadership.

> # Innovation can't come from experience

In most organizations, the innovative work is left to a select group of people in functions such as product development, marketing, engineering, or some other super-secret ninja lab. On the whole, this approach has been remarkably successful for those few workplaces that have been able to harness that creative force. But how much more successful could we be if we tapped the potential for innovative thinking in everyone working with us?

For leaders, this is where the real problems start. Drawing innovation out of people is hard. It requires taking them patiently through learning processes and by setting and enforcing new rules for work. It is time consuming, labor-intensive, and frustrating. It's like dragging someone through slop. But if you do it—if you make it through the slop—then the magic can happen. I've also learned that without the slop, there won't be any magic, ever. And without the magic, we won't stay in business. So keep reading, because this book will help you wade right in and start slogging.

AN INTEGRAL GOAL

The key goal of this book is to help workplaces cultivate a people-oriented philosophy that will serve as the basis for an integrated operating system.

Such a system, fueled by the continuous improvement of all its functions, creates and enhances value. Only customers can define value. The foundation for this is lean thinking, a philosophy based on the successful practices and behaviors associated with the Toyota Production System, and gaining inroads into all industries. I'll discuss ways to leverage lean principles to achieve this integral goal throughout this book, but for now let's break it down into its major components.

People

Without people, there is no workplace. "People oriented" means that the work we do is designed for learning, growth, and development, therefore for the benefit of people. Of course a business needs to generate profit and offer a return for its owners to reward their sacrifice/investment/risk. However, developing people and releasing their creativity and energy in defining new products and services, and in improving the processes for delivering those products and services to customers, not only generates more profit, but also attracts more talent to invest energy in the workplace. The same thing applies to workplaces that aren't driven by profit, since the ability to improve delivery of products and services, and thus reach a broader constituency, increases dramatically with a people-oriented focus.

Philosophy

Each of us has a personal philosophy, a way of thinking, of seeking wisdom, and of searching for truth. This philosophy, which we develop based on the set of experiences learned over a lifetime, both guides our behavior and reinforces our basic values. Those values influence everything we do, including what we do at work. When we get into the description of behavior a little later in this book, I will remind you that defining the values of your organization lays the foundation for the behavior you will get from those who work there. If you're not getting the behavior you want from your people (especially your leaders), it is probably because you either haven't articulated these values clearly enough or you have not put any teeth into a mechanism that requires the behavior described.

Integrated System

An integrated system means that everything within a workplace affects and is affected by everything else within the workplace. Organizations, like people, are collections of systems. Systems thinking tells us that every system (or process) is part of a larger system, and every system (or process) can be broken down into smaller systems. The human body contains the cardiovascular system, the skeletal system, the nervous system, and a hundred others. If any individual system fails, the whole body is in trouble because each system is integral to the whole. The same holds true for workplaces. If we make a change in one area, the effects will ripple through the rest of the system.

Value

Value is a function of what a product or service is worth to a customer and what it costs the customer. We want to do things in our workplaces that increase the worth (improve quality, deliver on time consistently, etc.) while driving down the cost of producing the product or delivering the service. Keep in mind that if you just drive down your costs but don't share some of the savings with your customers, you have not increased value, because you haven't made an impact on your customers' value equation.

Customer

Every workplace functions to serve some type of customer, but the term "customer" need not always refer to someone willing to pay for what you provide. A refugee in a camp in Africa is a customer for the aid organization. The salesperson is a customer for the payroll department. Regardless of whether someone is paying for the product or service they receive, value has to flow from the understanding of what a customer needs (which they may or may not know) and what they want (which they may or may not know). Understanding value depends on the ability of our workplace to build enough of a relationship with our customers to allow us to help them shape their understanding of what they need and want. An organization's ability to do this successfully reveals a lot about its values.

STRUCTURE

Each chapter in this book explores some facet of the elements discussed above.

Chapter 1 offers an organizing framework and foundational information for applying leadersights in a workplace.

Chapter 2 explores the value of vision and how to use your vision as a functional tool to drive continuous improvement.

Chapter 3 covers behavior and learning, discussing practical ways to tap into the power that everyone brings to work every day.

Chapter 4 introduces the concept of self-efficacy, arguably the most important foundational component for enabling a true culture of continuous improvement.

Chapter 5 dips into teams, team structure, and team leadership as well as how to effectively build teams and keep them going. The team structure is fundamental to making any of these other ideas work. Get this right, and things get easier. Get this wrong, and no matter how hard you work you'll fall short of creating a great workplace.

Chapter 6 describes "integral leadership," a new model of leadership that layers a variety of other well-known leadership styles to serve a workplace. We will explore ways to cultivate and integrate these styles and behaviors to become better leaders.

Chapters 7 and 8 focus on critical system tools that can bring high performance and satisfaction into the workplace. Chapter 7 provides some food for thought about the use of certain lean tools, from visual management to workplace organization. Chances are you've heard of and used these before, but in the spirit of kaizen, we'll look at them from a slightly different perspective to give you some ideas about making them easier to teach and use in developing people. Chapter 8 focuses on the importance of standardized work and how to use it to develop people and leaders in any type of workplace and doing any type of work.

Chapter 9 attempts to evolve the plan-do-check-act cycle, or PDCA, a proven process, but one I think we can improve, just like any other process. We'll push these ideas toward a truly rigorous learning system that I call the C4 process, one of significant importance for thriving in an unknown and unknowable future.

Finally, Chapter 10 provides a brief wrap-up for the leadersights of loving, learning, and letting go, and describes the Vigorous Learning

Organization in a little more detail. Ultimately, we challenge you to begin leading in a different way, focusing on people, and creating a great workplace; one that is the most effective, satisfying, and high-performing workplace you can imagine.

Please let me know where you run into roadblocks or really make something great. Challenge my ideas here and let's refine them in the fire of dialog.

1

The Framework

One of the best ways I've found to teach people about the components of a philosophy, lean in particular, is to compare the basic elements of that philosophy to something familiar to everyone, like the structural elements of a house—a foundation, the floor, two pillars, and the roof (see Figure 1.1). Unlike a real house, it seems to work better if we describe this one by building it from the top down instead of from the bottom up.

In the leadersights, or vigorous learning, philosophy, "customer satisfaction" serves as the roof, providing lasting shelter from the elements of a hostile global economy. We all know that without satisfied customers who continue to consume our products or services, and to tell other people about them, we won't survive in the market. "Just-in-time"—which represents the structural components that make our system work daily—and "Jidoka"—which represents the management systems that place the needs of people over the needs of machinery—form the structural and operating pillars of our system; they support the roof. Unless these two elements work together, we won't be able to produce or deliver effective results and the roof will collapse. It is important to note that in this two-dimensional (2D) metaphor, there are only two pillars. To have more would allow at least one to fail without the inevitable consequence of the roof collapsing. Both pillars have to be strong and both require continuous maintenance and improvement.

The floor and foundation represent the critical base of this sustainable framework. "Satisfaction" (on the job, for all employees, at all levels) is the floor; "dynamic stability" the foundation. These two chunks secure the future, and the subsequent chapters of this book will build a case for constructing them in actual workplaces. Without defining, nurturing, and improving the underlayment of satisfaction and dynamic stability, the system cannot survive. If the floor and the foundation are weak, the roof is going to come down no matter how strong the pillars.

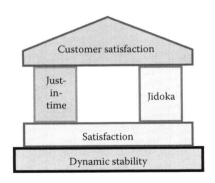

FIGURE 1.1
Framework.

SATISFACTION

Many people work under the assumption that a happy worker is a productive worker and that happiness and satisfaction are the same thing. We can probably make the argument for a similarity between happy and satisfied, since both are influenced by the same factors, but is a happy worker necessarily a productive worker?

Every workplace has people who seem to love being there. They show up every day and genuinely enjoy interacting with their coworkers, whom they view as friends. They're interested in catching up on everyone's weekend, college class, or anything else going on in life. They get along with everyone and everyone seems to like them, but they never seem to get any work done. There are also people in the same workplace who always appear to hate being there. They may enjoy the work, but if they do it's not apparent to anyone else because they always seem grumpy about something, usually about the amount of work assigned to them. Ironically, in many cases, leaders do give these particular people more work, knowing that such individuals will always get it done on time.

After about 70 years of research on job satisfaction, science still can't prove a causal link between satisfaction and productivity. Given this fact, many organizations have focused much more on productivity than on creating a workplace that is satisfying to those who work there. This attitude is most likely a remnant of designing work suitable for mass manufacturing.

Henry Ford began building cars in 1898. By 1908, when he introduced the Model T, he was one of 253 carmakers in North America. Originally, a team of men skilled in the various trades required would build each Model

T in its own work area. Those skills, of course, took time to develop but Ford's crews still built 10,607 Model Ts that year, selling them for about $850 each, a substantial sum of money at the time.

In those days, automobiles were expensive novelties for wealthy people, but Ford wanted to build a car "for the multitude." He knew demand would skyrocket if he could find the right mix of quality, simplicity, and price. But if demand were to skyrocket, how would he keep up with production? His solution, sparked by observing the work of Chicago's meat packers, was the moving assembly line.

In 1913, Ford's engineers rigged a simple moving assembly line at the company's new plant in Highland Park, Michigan. The line cut production time of the Model T from 12.5 to 5 hours, 50 minutes (Banham, p. 38). Ford had found his mix.

By 1914, the price of Ford's cars was going down and demand was going up, but the monotony of the work was grinding down his workers, causing many to leave. Ford's solution was to offer wages of $5 a day when the going rate for autoworkers was $11 a week. Applicants flocked to his door—a veritable Gold Rush of potential workers—from which Ford could select the most skilled and talented men to build his automobiles. The assembly line scheme, from a productivity standpoint, worked perfectly, and in 1916, Ford produced 730,041 Model Ts, selling them for about $360 each (Foner & Garraty, p. 409).

From a satisfaction standpoint, however, it was a disaster. Ford had taken highly skilled autoworkers and craftsmen—men used to building an entire car by themselves or with the help of just a few others—and assigned them a single task, like hanging a door, that they would do all day long. With their expertise no longer needed (or valued), these skilled workers got bored very quickly. When people get bored, their minds often wander, which leads to mistakes and other workplace troubles. To ensure workers stayed focused, Ford assigned foremen who often used abusive measures to keep workers on task. It's hardly surprising that his "solution" generated a substantial amount of animosity between labor and management, both at Ford and in other industries that employed the same tactics. The lingering result is a penetrating mistrust within the workplace that, sadly, persists in many places to this day.

The workers at Ford no longer had pride of ownership in their work. Any sense of autonomy these craftsmen may have enjoyed before the assembly line was introduced had disappeared; they couldn't even see the finished product. Instead, they spent all day working on a single component or subassembly. And because teaching someone how to do one of these small chunks of work took a matter of minutes instead of the years of training and qualification required in a skilled trade, any sense of job security that they had vanished as well.

On the plus side, they were getting paid $5 a day for a workday that was only 10 hours long. This left each man 14 hours each day to find something meaningful to do with his life. Today, of course, we voice such sentiments with more than a touch of sarcasm, but in the early twentieth century (and sometimes far beyond), there were many factory owners and others, Ford among them, who felt they were offering workers a fair deal, and that once a man had signed on as an employee, the employer had a right to use that man's labor at will in any way that would generate the highest profits.

In the days since the Model T, many companies have recognized how valuable employees are and have taken great strides to create engaging workplaces. Zappos.com is a perfect example. In its fulfillment center in Shepherdsville, Kentucky, Zappos called the employees "superheroes" because they were the ones who satisfy customers by overcoming adversity in the pursuit of truth, justice, and the American way. Superhero themes could be found throughout the fulfillment center. The company provided lunch to employees at no charge, and the 25-cent charge for vending machine items was collected and donated to local charities. The Zappos employees I met loved working there and it showed.

But free lunches and cheap snacks, along with the other benefits offered, are luxuries few companies can sustain. Any organization with short-term demands from stockholders or other owners has a very hard time justifying these types of expenses. Tony Hsieh, owner of Zappos.com, was able to do it because it was his money. Now that Amazon.com has taken over the Shepherdsville fulfillment center, many of these benefits have been done away with. What remains is the actual work.

Zappos.com and other organizations that have done great things for their people have focused primarily on the work *environment* as opposed to the work itself. They've acknowledged that work is mind-numbing and dull, so they induce people to stay by offering high wages and/or great benefits or by fostering a playful environment for when people aren't actually working.

What could we do if we focused on the *work* itself, instead of the environment? What if we made it possible for the work itself to bring the satisfaction that made people want to show up every day? This is my goal in writing this book—creating great leaders who create great workplaces.

If a happy worker is not necessarily a productive worker, then what *do* we get from satisfied employees that we don't get from those who are dissatisfied? First, a satisfied worker is more likely to want to come to work every day, so attendance tends to be better and turnover tends to be lower. But the real benefit comes in a satisfied worker's willingness to share his or her ideas for improving things in the workplace. Dissatisfied employees aren't averse to telling you what's on their minds, but they typically offer complaints rather than ideas. On the surface, it would seem these two types of workers are opposites, but the truth is a bit more complex. As we delve deeper, keep this thought in mind: satisfaction and dissatisfaction are not opposite ends of the same spectrum.

> ### Satisfaction and dissatisfaction are not opposite ends of the same spectrum

The satisfaction spectrum runs from satisfaction to no satisfaction. The dissatisfaction spectrum runs from dissatisfaction to no dissatisfaction. In every workplace, there are things that promote satisfaction and dissatisfaction, and these things are distinctly different. Psychologist Fredrick Herzberg wrote about these differences—what he called motivators and hygiene factors—in his article, "One more time: How do you motivate employees?" (*Harvard Business Review*, January–February 1968, with reprints and retrospective published September–October 1987, Reprint number 87507.)

One of Herzberg's key arguments is that you cannot motivate employees with money or by treating them well. You can only do so through factors related to the work. According to his research, true motivators are things like achievement, recognition, the work itself, and responsibility. These are what promote satisfaction.

> ### You cannot motivate employees with money or by treating them well

Hygiene factors—things that cause dissatisfaction—include company policies and administration, supervision, relationship with supervisors, and working conditions. If the policies or administration are compli-cated or fraught with red tape; if supervisors openly take credit for employees' ideas; if supervisors don't listen or support employees; or if working conditions are outright harsh, people are going to be dissatis-fied. On the other hand, just because policies are clear and easy, super-visors treat their employees with respect, and the work environment is clean and comfortable does not especially mean employees will be moti-vated to come to work. However, these things should keep from making employees angry.

My belief is that the root cause of all dissatisfaction in all workplaces is unresolved problems. This includes the unresolved problem of having a boss who's a jerk. The frustration of having to work around some problem that should be solvable, day after day, grinds people down. As we explore behaviors for leaders throughout the rest of this book, we'll keep coming back to the things that cause dissatisfaction and discuss certain things we can do about them, keeping in mind that the answers lie in solving people's unresolved problems.

> **The root cause of all dissatisfaction in all workplaces is unresolved problems**

Beyond Herzberg, findings from years of research generally point to three factors that have the biggest impact on job satisfaction as well as on overall satisfaction in life. These factors are meaningfulness, awareness, and responsibility.

Meaningfulness

As human beings, we seek meaningfulness for our lives, and because we spend so much time on the job, it's only logical for most of us to seek that meaning at work. However, like the simple tasks assigned to Henry Ford's highly skilled men, too many jobs today have been designed for productivity or efficiency, sacrificing meaningfulness to whatever it takes to increase the bottom line.

Meaningfulness has three primary components: significance, identity, and variety. We need to feel our purpose in life has significance, that it's important not only for us but for others as well. Too many people report they are trapped in meaningless jobs, and a slow economy compounds these feelings.

Identity defines who we are. We need to feel we belong to a particular group and that the people around us will look after us (and give us reasons to look after them). This sense of connection can take place at several levels. We can and often do take pride in the identity offered by a company and its brands. For example, respected companies like Apple, GE, and Berkshire Hathaway immediately give employees a strong, high-level identity. The next level might be classified by technical specialty or task identity such as design, engineering, purchasing, sales, or manufacturing. More often than not though, the strongest sense of identity comes from our teammates—the people with whom we work every day. We can feel great pride in working for Google or Coca-Cola, but if the people we have to interact with every day drive us crazy, our satisfaction levels are going to drop. This makes a team structure critical for success. We'll describe teams more fully in Chapter 5.

People like to have different things to do during the workday. Variety tends to make the day go faster and makes work more interesting, even if it involves no more than rotating from one assembly position to another in a factory. Many of us find satisfaction in the challenges associated with solving unanticipated problems. We might arrive at work with no plan except to wait for that phone call, email, or text message that something's on fire and we need to go stomp it out. This wreaks havoc on stability, but it is very engaging for many people, particularly those in otherwise boring management positions. This is one of the reasons people resist stability-enhancing workplace improvements.

Leadersights: Loving

Boost feelings of significance by drawing a closer connection between your customers and your employees. Even something as simple as posting in the workstation a picture of your completed product in use will help people draw the connection between their work and the customer. Publicize customer feedback, and not just the bad comments. Share the good ones. Invite customers to visit your facility and allow them to interact with your people. Reward your people with visits to customer locations.

Awareness

The more people know about what's going on within their organization, the more likely they are to report higher levels of satisfaction. While our leaders' expectations of us are likely the most important things we need to know, our satisfaction levels are tied more to the feedback we get from them rather than to the clarity of those expectations. Knowing the expectations is one thing, but knowing whether we are meeting those expectations seems to correlate more with satisfaction. As human beings, we tend to under-communicate what we expect from those around us, often assuming they will just "know" how we feel and what we want in a given situation. When we provide new employees with a thick stack of procedures and then have someone show them the ropes, we honestly believe we've fully communicated our expectations. Anyone who has ever been a new employee can attest to the insufficiency of this approach, yet most employers continue to rely on it. This thinking has to change. Leaders have to design work with satisfaction in mind and keep that as important as productive efficiency.

Leaders need to become experts at communicating their own expectations, but must also understand what their people expect of them. Once these critical lines of two-way communication are established, it's important for each party to continually confirm that they are meeting the other's expectations. This type of interchange is challenging in even our most intimate relationships. How often do arguments between spouses result from unstated expectations? In a work environment where we don't know other people as well as we probably should, the task is often overwhelming.

Leadersights: Learning

Boost awareness through visual management systems that clearly show the daily goals and their progress toward those goals. I've included some details in Chapter 7.

Responsibility

All the research conducted on satisfaction over the years has concluded that feelings of responsibility promote feelings of satisfaction, yet when most people are asked to accept more responsibility, their typical response is either a flat "no" or a question about more money. Since this response is seen in workplaces around the world, it's obvious that the most common way managers give people more responsibility is by giving them more work to do. What leaders need to do instead is design work that increases *feelings* of responsibility among their workers, without overburdening them.

Feelings of responsibility result from autonomy and control. When people believe they can do something about conditions in their workplace, they are usually more satisfied. This doesn't mean leaders should just turn over control of the workplace to the workforce and hope for the best. But it does mean leaders should put systems in place that channel employee creativity and that give both parties—leaders and employees alike—a strong feeling of control. One such system is the C4 process, which is described in detail in Chapter 9.

As always, today's leaders are responsible for results, and they're under constant time pressure to deliver them. Those who succeed regardless of the barriers are often tapped for promotion, but by focusing on these criteria alone, we often reward "do-it-yourself" behavior. Leaders become accustomed to completing tasks on their own because they don't have time to teach their people how to get the same results they get by doing the task themselves. People are thus left with trivial tasks so leaders don't have to risk allowing them to do more important work. If we design work to mitigate the risks to leaders, we'll begin to see more productive and satisfying work in the hands of people throughout our organizations. In Chapter 5, we take on this task directly.

Leadersights: Loving

Fix inequities in your compensation system. Good pay won't motivate anyone to do better work, but crappy pay will certainly motivate them to find work elsewhere, or make sure they only give enough effort to keep from getting fired. Eliminate this problem now by making wages and salaries more competitive externally and perfectly equitable internally. People working for you should be paid well in comparison with others in the local area, and people doing similar work should get similar pay. Otherwise, you continually run the risk of losing them.

Changing a compensation system is not something for the faint of heart. Pull focus groups of employees together to develop a detailed understanding of pay perceptions, and then ask them for ideas. Try to keep the system as flat as possible. (Multiple pay grades for different work classifications increase the likelihood someone will be asked to do something he or she didn't expect to have to do. Then the grumbling starts.)

Take your time and get it right, and don't be afraid to hire some compensation experts if you think you need to. One firm, for example, took 2 years to change from an 80-year-old, piece-rate compensation system to a modern hourly system, but the time invested was well worth it.

DYNAMIC STABILITY

Dynamic stability is the foundation of the leadersights framework. It is what connects the organization to its grounded values, the most important things the workplace wants to be. In another context, we might not think of these two words ("dynamic" and "stability") as going together, but they provide an accurate description of what today's workplaces need, and form the basis upon which everything else in the framework rests.

Every workplace needs things that don't change without deliberate and thoughtful action. Stability—consistency, repeatability, regularity, and predictability—allows us to design work for people so that everyone knows what to do. Stability also allows us to more accurately balance work. Finally, stability is absolutely essential for building skills (we have to repeat the way we work to get better).

At the same time we create stability, however, we also need to be dynamic—flexible and responsive to things that change constantly. When we're dynamic, we can respond quickly to changing customer demands, shortages in components or other raw materials, an absent team member, breakdowns in equipment, and other problems. The primary goal under leadersights is to create a workplace that operates with perfectly stable processes but can change instantly based on the needs of the customer.

The concept of dynamic stability requires some thinking to get one's head around. I've been thinking about this for years, and I'm still searching for answers, but I've concluded (so far) that dynamic stability results much more from leadership and leader behaviors than anything else. Even then, leadership by itself is insufficient. Leadership—particularly the leadership mindset—must be combined with learning, a team-based work structure, empowerment, and trust to create the foundation of dynamic stability.

Leadership Mindset

What shapes the effective leader's mindset? What should shape his or her mindset? First up is the recognition that workplaces exist to serve some customer's need. Founders and owners of business organizations typically benefit from satisfying this need and thus are motivated to continue to do so. The process of establishing, understanding, and communicating this proposition forms the core of the workplace. This defines the concept of the "value proposition."

When Jim Collins wrote "Good to Great," a study of what it takes for companies to achieve and sustain outstanding results, one thing he talked about was the hedgehog concept. The hedgehog is the intersection of the things you do best with the things you can make money doing. Collins then added a third input: the things you do best and can make money doing should also be things you love to do (remember the importance of satisfaction?). If your value proposition allows you to make money by doing the things you do better than anyone else because you love doing them, then your foundation is set.

Both the founders of new companies and the CEOs of old ones need to be able to project an image of their organization into the future. Before there's a value proposition, there's a vision. We'll talk more about this in Chapter 2, but for now recognize that vision is the main motivator for long-term behavior, because vision is what attracts people and keeps them working.

From the value proposition and the vision flow the organization's values. Values tell people what behaviors are required in the workplace, but the only way to make these values meaningful is to build strategic goals and plans focused on advancing them. For example, to proclaim "integrity" as a value and then tolerate known instances of lying to others, especially to customers, establishes a structure of mistrust that undermines any other effort. We'll break down values further in Chapter 3.

If the workplace requirements for behavior are determined by its values, then the culture is established by the commitment of its people to live by those values. Commitment has to be visible, and it has to be substantive. My favorite story about commitment is one I heard years ago from a teacher in the army about a country breakfast of ham and eggs. To make that breakfast, the teacher pointed out, the chicken makes a contribution, but the pig makes a commitment.

How does all this translate to leaders? To drive a workplace to higher and higher levels of performance requires much more than simply doing a relatively narrowly defined job. Leaders must be seen as modeling proper behaviors. People will mimic the behaviors of their leaders when they feel there is a compelling reason to do so. If a leader's efforts are halfhearted, however, why should anyone else give his or her all to make something happen?

In the early stages of any organizational change, most people agree that everyone in the workplace must be committed to the change to make it stick. This may be true, but for workplaces where years of mistrust have forged fragile relationships between people and their leaders (and that's most of them), the only commitment we can reasonably expect from the workforce is to show up. Yes, we want their ideas. Yes, we want their involvement. But unless they come to work consistently, we can't teach them. If they're not there, we can't listen to their ideas and they can't be involved. To get employees to want to come to work, we have to create a work environment that builds satisfaction. That is why each chapter in this book ultimately ties back to satisfaction and its importance to a thriving workplace.

The last element in shaping the leader's mindset is discipline. For most of us, discipline conjures up a mental image of punishment. "Failure to arrive on time will result in ...*fill in punishment here*." But the word has multiple meanings, and most of the other meanings are related to learning. Even the root of the word is revealing, because it is shared with the word disciple. When asked to define "disciple," most people answer "follower," but this is not exactly true. Yes, disciples follow, but they follow a leader (teacher, mentor, master, rabbi, imam, etc.) because they want to learn from that person. And they want to learn because they believe in the outcome (the vision) offered by that leader. The greatest learning value comes when the leader turns the tables and requires the disciples to go out and teach others what they have learned.

Discipline requires that leaders develop people by teaching them, and the best way to ensure people understand what they've been taught is for them to teach others. A number of organizations have embraced this truth, which is why we've seen mentoring programs flourish. We've also seen such programs wither, because mentoring or teaching or coaching is not something we can casually add to a leader's list of things to do. To me, teaching to develop people is the most important function a leader performs. Learning to do so properly and effectively is a set of skills that requires careful development. The remaining chapters will help to teach you how to build those skills.

> Teaching to develop
> people is the most
> important function a
> leader performs

In summary, what are the concepts that should shape a leader's mindset?

Value
Vision
Values
Commitment
Discipline

Learning and Situational Awareness

Building dynamic stability also requires the creation and maintenance of rigorous organizational learning systems. A learning organization is one that promotes the development of individual skills to the level of mastery for everyone in the workplace. Developing individual skills toward mastery is a function of work, not of training. Training can get things started, but mastery is only attainable through repetition and focused corrective feedback.

Learning, even for individuals, is a collective activity. It takes at least two people in some kind of relationship to create learning. This could be as simple as the author of a book and the reader, but if it is to be meaningful, learning usually shows up in behavior and interaction with others. If you're a golfer and you practice for endless hours by yourself, then play a course by yourself and achieve a score of par, that's an individual accomplishment that reflects learning and you can take pride in it. But aren't you going to tell somebody else about it? Isn't golf usually more fun when you play against/with other players? Don't you pick up tips about your swing, your club selection, or your short game by watching your opponents? It is interaction that solidifies learning and makes it mean something.

> Interaction solidifies
> learning and makes it
> mean something

When building a foundation of dynamic stability, the workplace needs to focus its learning abilities to be more externally competitive. The way it defines both its strategic niche in the marketplace and its operating environment is critical to understanding what work must be done in order to succeed—and how well. The operating environment includes space to actively influence what happens (the area of influence) as well as space that might provide new threats or opportunities (the area of interest). To foster the greatest area of interest, the organization must continually scan the environment to seek new opportunities.

The best description of this concept I have read recently is in "Great by Choice," where authors Jim Collins and Morton Hansen discuss the difference between shooting bullets and shooting cannons. To learn what is going on in your operating environment, you have to try things, or probe until you find something to work with. The initial opportunities you identify represent bullets. They are small and cheap, so you fire a lot of them in a several different directions to learn what's out there and assess what happens next. When you hit something, you shoot again to confirm (experiment to reproduce the effect). Then, when you're confident you've identified a significant opportunity, you load up the cannon and shoot the big stuff (e.g., put serious resources behind a new product launch after all the focus groups have shown that the product will be a hit).

The most important aspect of learning within a workplace is the work. Seeking to understand the work will always be a priority activity. It sounds simple enough, but to do so requires leaders to acknowledge that they don't understand the work. In most workplaces, if leaders were to actually do this—confess openly that they didn't understand the work their people were doing—not only would it reflect incompetence, but also probably end their careers. Work, however, is not so simple.

Things happen every day, sometimes every hour, that people have to work around, power through, fix, move, modify, throw away, clean, tighten, edit, rework, etc. However, if leaders aren't where the action is, actively seeking to understand the work, they'll never observe these challenges, the vast majority of which have nothing to do with written job instructions. How much time leaders spend every day in the physical workspace learning, coaching, supporting, correcting, experimenting, encouraging, helping, etc., is not the kind of thing we typically evaluate their performance on, is it? But it's an easy key performance indicator to measure, and it works in shaping leader behaviors.

Leaders of learning organizations lead and learn in the workplace, not in offices.

Team Structure and Empowering the Workforce

Empowerment has long been a recommended strategy for leaders. Recently, a client in the aerospace industry listed all the management or change initiatives on which the company had spent over $100,000 in the past 20 years. There were 53 of them! More than likely, most of them included something about empowering the workforce.

Business- and/or leadership-oriented magazine articles, books, and presentations constantly remind us to empower, empower, empower. Why all these reminders? Because for leaders, empowering is risky business, and most of them fail miserably at what seems like a simple task. Leaders have responsibility for outcomes, good or bad, regardless of who does the work. If they aren't confident their subordinates can do the work with the same speed and quality they can, they are neither likely to empower their people nor take the time to teach them to do better. But if no one except the leader knows how to do the task well, what happens to the future of the organization?

Empowering requires changes to the structure of work and changes in how leaders are evaluated. Until we have systems in place that compel leaders to spend more time teaching and coaching and less time "doing," the workforce will never be empowered. That structure is a relatively small team. If we expect leaders to challenge, support, correct, and encourage people, we have to realize that there are limits to our human capability to do that. It is impossible to provide that kind of coaching support to very many people. Our workplaces have to be structured in a way that allows these leaders to exhibit the proper behaviors, and that means organizing around small teams. Hundreds of studies have been carried out on teams and none has the definitive answer on team size. We will discuss teams further in Chapter 5, but for now, know that the entire organization, from the CEO to the value creators, should be on teams of four to six people with a leader in a supporting and coaching role, and not necessarily in the "boss" role.

Building Trust: Clear Expectations and Vulnerability

Relationships between the people doing the work and the people managing the workplace are critical in any workplace, and balancing these relationships has been a challenge for at least 110 years. Through a history of scientific management, endless productivity improvements, incentive structures, piece-rate quotas, and maximizing shareholder wealth, leaders have managed to turn work into something that usually sucks. With every layoff, every labor rate cut, and every bonus paid to the CEO, we take a little bite out of trust. Is it surprising that in most workplaces a huge trust gap exists between labor and management? There are trust gaps between departments in the same organization. There are trust gaps between suppliers and customers. In too many places I've visited, management was oblivious of this fact, or believed it was an unchangeable aspect of their organization. Most are convinced they are trusted and loved by their people.

Everyone has had personal experience with building trust and violating trust, whether it was having a grade school friend rat you out to the teacher or having a fight with your spouse because you were supposed to know he or she hated the movie you rented. Most supervisor courses teach new leaders that, to build trust, they must be consistent and treat everyone the same way. Building trust is more than just a set of dictates universally applied. It's a two-way street; a relationship.

There are two key components to the business of trust building: clear expectations and vulnerability.

Clear Expectations

To begin with, each party in the relationship has to clarify their expectations of the other. In our most intimate relationships, we assume the other knows us well enough, so we don't put much effort into ensuring they understand exactly what we expect of them (though there are times when we wish we'd tried a little harder). At work, of course, it's much more difficult to clarify our expectations, even with a variety of communication tools at our disposal. Despite mechanisms ranging from job descriptions to employee newsletters to team information boards, the biggest complaint on employee surveys is lack of communication. It probably isn't the leader that messes this up; more likely it's the imperfect information available to the leader, combined with the lack of trust that exists in the first place. Remember, effective communication is first and foremost a function of trust.

> **Effective communication is a function of trust**

In the absence of trust, information gaps are filled in with anything employees can think of, and rumors start and persist, even in mature organizations. Here's a perfect example: after compressing the working footprint of a few manufacturing cells at a client site, the workers told me that the last time they saw floor space cleared up was because some of the work was moved to their factory in Mexico. Naturally, they assumed we were there to move more work to Mexico, and once that assumption spread to nearly everyone, our job (making space for new product lines) became much more challenging. I even had a friend who was a team member at Toyota Motor Manufacturing in Kentucky who asked me if I thought they were trying to get "the union" into Toyota when a change to the suggestion system happened at the same time a new president took over. No workplace is exempt from this challenge.

Most of the communication tools available to leaders are limited to reflecting the leaders' expectations of subordinates. For example, we promote standardized work as a critical tool for a lean workplace. Standardized work unequivocally spells out the company's expectations of people working in a given position. We often post the standardized work for everyone to see. But as leaders, what must we do to make sure *we* understand our team members' expectations of us?

One thing we can do is to create our own Leader Standardized Work (LSW) and post it publicly in the work area. Chapter 8 contains some ideas about preparing LSW, but above all we, as leaders, have to listen carefully to the expectations of our team members. Once the expectations of leaders and workers are clear in both directions, both parties need to work at satisfying them.

Vulnerability

In my view, a leader's unwillingness to be vulnerable to the performance of his or her employees is the primary reason empowerment fails. Many people associate vulnerability with weakness, and we are taught throughout our lives to avoid letting others (especially competitors) see our weaknesses. So it is not surprising that some people think leaders must project an image of invulnerability or risk losing the respect of their employees. In reality, it isn't our image we need to worry about; it's our sanity. Unless we can get some help from the people who work with us, we'll go crazy trying to do everything that must be done.

Because of the perceived risk of making ourselves vulnerable, we need to experiment; to try on this new role in small ways and in controlled circumstances until we find out for sure what will happen. But we must begin to rethink this idea, because if we can't let our guard down around our teammates, work can really be stressful, not just for leaders but also for all levels of employees. Teams must build trust the same way, because without trust, teams never really become teams.

Leadersights: Letting Go

Vulnerability means we let other people know a little bit more about us—who we are, what we like, and what we know. To get new (or not so new) groups to start down the road to becoming teams, have them do a PIG Personality Profile, a fun assessment developed by Gordon Cotton, a trainer at Marine Atlantic, Inc., in New Brunswick, Canada.

Purpose. Participants get to know themselves in a fun way.

Step 1. Have everyone draw a picture of a pig on a clean sheet of paper. Remind them that the way they draw the pig reflects their personality, whether they know it or not.

Step 2. After everyone has finished drawing their pig, tell them they can interpret themselves in the following ways:

- If the pig is drawn on the top portion of the page, you are generally optimistic and positive
- If the pig is drawn in the middle of the page, you are realistic and factual
- If the pig is drawn toward the bottom of the page, you are pessimistic or tend to be negative
- If the pig is facing left, you are traditional, friendly, and usually remember important events and dates
- If the pig is facing right, you are innovative and action oriented but not family or date oriented
- If the pig is facing straight ahead (looking at you), you are direct, like to play devil's advocate, and don't avoid issues
- If the body of the pig is facing one direction but its head is turned so that it's facing you, you may have bigger issues and should seek professional help
- If the pig is very detailed (relative to the amount of time you spent drawing), you are analytical, cautious, and suspicious

- If the pig has little detail, you are a risk taker, emotional, and bored by detail
- If the pig has four feet, you are secure, stubborn, and have firm beliefs
- If the pig has fewer than four feet, you are either generally insecure or you're going through major changes in life
- The larger the pig's ears, the better listener you are
- And last, but not least, the length of the pig's tail represents the quality of your sex life

This exercise may not be scientific, but it always gets a few laughs. It also gives us a playful and nonthreatening way to begin to talk about ourselves in a nonwork context, and that opens a small window to our souls and makes us just a little bit vulnerable.

CHAPTER SUMMARY

House metaphor for the leadersights framework:

- Roof = Customer satisfaction (the goals of the workplace)
- Pillars = Just-in-time and Jidoka (the operating structure and management systems we build for the daily work we do)
- Floor = Satisfaction (for leaders and team members)
- Foundation = Dynamic stability (the piece that connects the workplace to the truly important outcomes we desire)

Components of satisfaction:

- Meaningfulness
  - Significance
  - Identity
  - Variety
- Awareness
  - Expectations (or standards)
  - Feedback (or status)

- Responsibility
  - Autonomy
  - Control

Components of dynamic stability:

- Leader's mindset
  - Value (value from the customer's perspective)
  - Vision
  - Values (the most important behaviors you want from your people)
  - Commitment
  - Discipline
- Learning and situational awareness
- Team structure and empowering the workforce
- Building trust
  - Clear expectations
  - Vulnerability

2

Vision and Metavision: Seeing the Whole before Setting the Strategy

Every workplace has a unique operating philosophy. Three major components of that philosophy (even if they have never been formally written down) are vision, mission, and values. This combination (for better or worse) drives everything the organization does.

Unfortunately, many people think of crafting a vision statement as an unnecessary exercise of little practical value. Even worse, these naysayers are correct way too often. If the vision is viewed as no more than a short paragraph on a website or a poster on a wall, rather than as a concrete goal to work toward every day, the time people spend putting it together is the time they can't afford to waste.

In this chapter, we're going to explore the impact of a positive, motivational vision statement. We're also going to introduce the idea of *metavision*, which in actuality has little to do with "vision" and everything to do with seeing and understanding the relationships that exist in workplaces.

As I continue to work with people in all kinds of workplaces, and at all different levels, it's becoming clearer to me that, for most people, their largest priority is whatever is currently happening. In today's pressing environment of greater complexity, competition, and demanding customers, stopping to define the future of the organization can seem like a distraction from today's urgent needs. And yet, exactly the opposite is true. If we fail to design the organization's future so that we can take steps to get there, we're putting ourselves at even greater risk.

THE PURPOSE OF VISION

An organizational vision has two purposes:

1. Motivating people
2. Giving people hope

A clear vision brings people together, so defining it is far more than an academic exercise. By providing a shared purpose for everyone, vision should help to create meaningfulness—something people want to pursue.

In Chapter 1, we talked about the importance of meaningfulness in creating a satisfying workplace. A vision your employees understand and believe in promotes teamwork, cooperation, collaboration, and camaraderie. It will guide strategy development and decision making throughout the workplace, and will drive people to achieve. In a nutshell, vision provides a framework through which we define our values. This is also an opportunity for business leaders to show people that the company stands for something other than just money.

A well-defined vision gives people the distinct feeling that things are getting (or will get) better, not worse. It lets everyone know that despite current conditions, we're committed to sticking it out together and succeeding, come what may. People should see or hear the vision and say, "I want to go there, too!"

Leadersights: Learning

Take a look at your company's vision statement or operating philosophy. If, after reading it, you can honestly say, "I want to be a part of that," please send it to me. If all you can say is something like "That's not too bad…," then do something about it. Create a new vision using the guidelines in this chapter.

Setting the right vision for an organization begins with understanding the organization's potential. You have to understand exactly what your people can do, what assets are available, and where team members can leverage those assets to reach higher levels of performance. In short, we need to see the whole of the organization.

METAVISION: SEEING THE WHOLE

Metavision is the ability to see a situation from multiple perspectives. It is the skill of understanding the likely impact on the connected pieces of the workplace when unpredictable events occur. All of us have some degree of foresight, but effective leaders see a picture of what kind of future is possible and then take deliberate steps to create that future in the face of a variety of obstacles. One of the skills we need to build is looking at our impact on the world, rather than always focusing on the world's impact on us.

Leadersights: Metavision

To begin building the skill of metavision, try this exercise. Visualize yourself in the center of a circle representing your work life. Surrounding the circle are the other pieces of the workplace and your life outside of work:

- Different departments
- The leadership team
- The board of directors
- Your competitors
- Your customers
- Your coworkers (includes your peers, people above you, and people below you)
- Your suppliers (including the folks who restock your vending machines and empty your trash cans, and the people from whom you buy office supplies)
- Your stockholders or other owners or potential owners
- Your community
- Your family

Now list the important factors that shape others' perceptions of your workplace:

- Design
- Customer relationships
- Manufacturing

- Innovation
- Project management
- Marketing
- Communications
- Information
- Employee skills and engagement
- Service level, etc.

Finally, list the factors that are important for your future:

- Financial
- Operational
- Environmental—consumption of water, energy, and materials
- Health and wellness of the workforce and community
- Security
- Air and water quality, etc.

Once you have all this on paper, systematically work your way through every stakeholder, drawing connections between each of them and your workplace. Also note connections between and among other stakeholders. When you're finished, consider the questions—or perception factors—listed below for each connection you've identified.

- How do we affect them now?
- How should we affect them in the future?
- What can we do to make it easier for them to interact with us?
- How do they affect us now?
- How should they affect us in the future?
- What can we do to make it easier for us to interact with them?

Each of these perception factors serves as a filter for your thinking process. After you've considered them for each individual connection, take the next step by working to close those connections or make them tighter. Take interacting with HR, for example. Ask, "from a security perspective, how does my group affect human resources?" Maybe you require some security screening prior to a hiring decision. Maybe you just need a new badge issued. Whatever the case, identify the information you need to give human resources for each connection (number of people required, skill set(s) required, time frame needed, for which department(s), full-time or temporary, etc.). Now note what information human resources should provide to you (people in the candidate pool, names of interviewers, when and where interviews are scheduled, interviewer guides—including applicant information, candidate report forms, etc.). Use this knowledge to organize the workplace in such a way that responses to any new requirements can be generated simply and easily.

The point of this exercise is to understand that when something happens at point *x* in your organization, you can expect what will happen in response at point *y* somewhere else. This type of analysis will allow you to anticipate the needs and requirements on both sides so that you can develop a plan to prepare team members.

The above exercise is a "slow-thinking" activity, but it's designed to prepare you for "fast thinking." No matter what the topic, we almost always start off learning in a slow, deliberate fashion, but with practice and experience, we're soon able to learn immediately and act automatically. Fighter pilots in air-to-air combat are the best example of this principle. When an enemy jet with armed missiles is closing in at Mach 2, there's not much time to analyze what's happening, synthesize a solution, evaluate that solution, and act upon it. To prepare themselves for these fleeting moments, pilots spend thousands of hours in slow-learning activities and simulations.

The information you gather through metavision not only allows you to shape a vision that takes into account the complex relationships within a workplace, but also helps you gain better buy-in from the people on your team.

This clear understanding of the workplace and its potential shapes your thinking for creating a more effective vision. The vision, however, shouldn't be limited by the assessment. Rather, it should tell you what steps you'll need to take, what changes you'll need to make, and what direction you'll need to go early on in the pursuit of that vision.

VISION AND MISSION

Vision is what you want to become. Mission is what you do every day to get there. Therefore, your mission is to achieve your vision.

> # Your Mission is to achieve your Vision

In the 1980s, during my career as an army officer, I served as a company commander in an infantry unit in Europe. Every day we trained for a war against the Soviet Union, and as part of that training, we spent a lot of time developing detailed plans for the unit's next specific mission. Every one of these plans—called operations orders (OPORDs)—followed the same five-paragraph format:

- *Situation.* Provides information about the enemy, friendly forces, and any other assets available for the unit.
- *Mission.* Describes what the unit must do. Includes who, what, when, where, and why.
- *Execution.* Describes how the unit will accomplish its mission. This includes the commander's intent and concept of the operation, unit assignments, and coordinating instructions.
- *Service support.* Provides details on all logistics affecting the mission.
- *Command and signal.* Describes who's in charge and the succession of leadership, the communication requirements, and any special instructions.

We never did anything without an OPORD, and the same format is also useful in civilian life for things like team charters and program management. Let's focus on the mission and concept of the operation. The concept of the operation can be considered the vision of the leader for this particular mission.

The mission again, spells out what the unit is supposed to do, specifying who, what, when, where, and why. For example:

"Second Platoon, B Company attacks to seize the western flank of Hill 452 NB12345678 NLT 140400ZJan14 to secure the left flank of B Company's overwatch position."

In this case:

- The who is the Second Platoon, B Company
- The what is attacking to seize
- The where is the western flank of Hill 452 NB12345678
- The when is NLT 140400ZJan14
- The why is to secure the left flank of B Company's overwatch position

The leader—regardless of his or her operating level, from team leader (TL) to commander-in-chief—also needs to spell out the *commander's intent* for his or her unit and for the next two levels up (e.g., an OPORD for a platoon also includes the commander's intent for the company commander and the battalion commander). The commander's intent, again, is the **vision** for a **particular** operation. It says in simple language, as if telling a story, where the unit wants to be when the operation is finished. For example:

> B Company will occupy Hill 452 as part of 4th Battalion's mission to pro-
> vide security and support to First Brigade's river crossing. 4th battalion
> will occupy Hills 452 and 481 and the ridgeline between them with tanks
> and artillery covering the high ground on the far side of the river. Infantry
> will secure the flanks and patrol the bridge abutments.

We want to let the soldiers know that, no matter what else happens, at the end of the day, we're going to be on that hill to make sure First Brigade can cross the river safely. This is the picture of where we want to be. Both the commander's intent and the mission have a specific goal in mind, but the intent always includes the bigger picture.

A vision statement paints a clear picture of the organization's future, giving it something specific to work toward, what it aims to become. A mission statement, on the other hand, tells everyone what the organization does every day to serve customers and stay in business while it simultaneously pursues the vision. Consider another way to think about the difference; the vision is for your people, the mission is for your customers (including stakeholders). The vision should get your people fired up to go forward. The mission tells customers that you're the right place to buy something from.

My favorite vision statement came from Walt Disney World (WDW) a few years ago:

> Walt Disney World will always be dedicated to making dreams come true. In
> this magical world, fantasy is real and reality is fantastic! A wonderful sense
> of community awaits, where all are greeted as welcome guests and become
> cherished friends. For all who work and play here, Walt Disney World will be
> a source of joy and inspiration (Handout provided in "The Disney Approach
> to Leadership Excellence" offered by The Disney Institute, 2001).

For the record, I have not been able to find this vision statement on any of Disney's websites or in their annual reports. It is, however, included in Lee Cockerell's *Creating Magic: 10 Common Sense Leadership Strategies from a Life at Disney* (Crown Business Press, October 2008) and on several fan websites.

I like this vision statement because it describes the type of organization Disney wants to create in this particular business unit. Who doesn't want to be a cherished friend and draw joy and inspiration from your workplace? It honestly makes me want to work there, and that's the intended effect. Notice that it doesn't say Disney wants to be the provider of choice for theme-park entertainment, or that it wants to be number 1 or 2 in every operating segment. This distinction is important, because your vision should focus on the future, not on your current products or position in the market. An effective vision tells a story about the kind of workplace you want to create in a way specific enough for people to make sense of it.

From a technical point of view, I could argue that the WDW vision is a nice, fluffy, meatless, and wordy statement. But that's okay, because vision does not stand alone. In fact, the very next step after creating a vision is to articulate the operational goals that will allow you to achieve it. In the case of Disney, what specifically are they planning to do to inspire people and bring joy? How do they measure and track those goals so they know they're making progress?

Another example I like is NASA's 2009 vision/mission combination, written before the budget for manned space exploration fell victim to our recent economic woes.

"At the core of NASA's future space exploration is a return to the moon, where we will build a sustainable long term human presence" (http://www.nasa.gov/about/exploration/home/index.html. October 2009—no longer available on the web).

Here, we see a clear goal of returning to the moon; a goal Jim Collins would call a Big Hairy Audacious Goal (BHAG). The best vision statements include a BHAG, because they give everyone something concrete on which to focus. If everyone sees the benefit of achieving the BHAG, they are more likely to work toward it. The BHAG also places a time horizon on accomplishing the vision. As soon as you achieve the BHAG, you need a new vision. That's healthy, too, since it makes vision an integral part of an achievement-oriented system, rather than simply a fancy plaque in the lobby.

NASA's mission statement provides a good example of what the organization did every day to make progress toward that vision:

> To pioneer the future in space exploration, scientific discovery and aeronautics research (http://www.nasa.gov/about/highlights/what_does_nasa_do.html. October 2009—this site is still available but has changed substantially to reflect NASA's new mission-oriented directorate structure).

Some companies like short catchphrases that allow people to remember their vision more easily. Such phrases often work to engage customers as well. For example, Skretting Australia, a manufacturer of fish feed, published its vision as "Feeding your passion for fish." Boston Consulting Group (number 3 on *Fortune* magazine's "100 Best Companies to Work For" in 2016) uses "Shaping the future together." These statements will likely need additional explication for the workforce so that everyone understands the intent, but they're short and snappy and people can relate to and remember them.

Leadersights: Learning

Create an effective working vision for your workplace. The vision could be the product of a single leader who is passionate about a new business. It could be the product of a small group within a leadership team who shape a vision together and then share it with their people. It also could be the product of focus groups within the workplace. If you already have a workable mission statement that people use every day to describe what they do at work, then use it to forecast your vision. What are you working toward?

The source of the vision doesn't matter. What matters is that it becomes a living, daily goal; one that shapes every other decision you make about the workplace and its future.

You're going to need a relatively impartial and skilled facilitator to help your team muddle through the creation of your new vision, so check around and see who might have this skill set and ask them to help.

Remember, the purpose of a vision is to provide hope, and to motivate behavior so that everyone is working toward a common goal. Here's an example: the vision statement below is pretty soft, so let's try to build it into a robust statement designed to motivate people to action:

> We will be a company of inspired people focused on creating high value, helping each other, and building a great organization.

This statement could apply to almost any organization, doing anything, anywhere. It sounds laudable but is way too generic to be a useful motivator. So what can we do to start making it more useful?

Let's start with "inspired people focused on creating high value." "Creating high value" is the key component here, because it both addresses customer need and drives the organization's financial success. If we add a dash of specificity related to products (or prospects) for the future, "creating high value" might morph into something like "developing an affordable 200-mpg engine," "finding the cure for Alzheimer's," or "harnessing the sun for powering communities." All of a sudden, a nice-sounding platitude has become a BHAG everyone can see as valuable and important. It's also something quantifiable that we can measure to determine progress.

Now, let's look at "inspired people." What inspires people? Positive contributions to society inspire people. Pulling together to overcome adversity inspires people. Winning inspires people, especially when the loser is obviously evil. By defining a BHAG and developing a system for tracking progress toward it, companies have a chance to be inspirational. But as with any other goal, it takes specificity to get people going. Don't limit yourself to your current experience base when defining a BHAG. If your BHAG is something as mundane as "becoming the provider of choice in x market" or "achieving a 14% market share," you're unlikely to motivate more than a small group of relatively shortsighted people.

Another way to look at inspiring people goes directly back to the discussion about satisfaction. If people are doing work they consider significant; if they are aware of expectations and their progress in meeting them; and if they have a sense of responsibility for achieving a goal, they are much more likely to be inspired than if none of the above is present.

Lastly, we need to look at the term "great organization." There are dozens of diagnostic or assessment instruments available by which organizations can measure their "greatness." The Malcolm Baldrige National Quality Award, TS 16949, the Shingo Prize for Operational Excellence, and others have their own standards for greatness. And, there are always new sustainability indexes, customer and employee surveys, competitive analyses, and consultants by the dozen to help organizations discover where they are in relation to other organizations. But before you sign up for the latest and greatest assessment tool, you first have to define what "a great organization" means to you. The answer could be as easy as "We want to be in the top ten on Fortune magazine's 'World's Most Admired Companies' and '100 Best Companies to Work For.'" Goals like these send a clear message to your team: let's do whatever it takes to make this a great company, but we all have to work together to get there.

So the vision statement may change from:

> "We will be a company of inspired people focused on creating high value, helping each other, and building a great organization," to:

> "We will be one of the world's 100 best companies, growing inspired people, helping each other pursue life-changing technologies for our customers. We seek ways to transport people to their important events in the safest, fastest, and cleanest manner possible."

An organization doesn't necessarily have to be big to be great, but it does have to be successful. It has to create the type of work environment that attracts and retains talent. And, it has to contribute to the community. Ask your employees what they think defines greatness for a workplace like yours, and then work their ideas into your vision discussion.

TYING BEHAVIOR TO THE MISSION

Remember, the vision of an organization sets the direction for its future. The mission explains what the organization does every day to achieve that vision. We must define the behaviors we want from people, particularly leaders. In working with groups, it is remarkably difficult to articulate these behaviors. In the platoon's mission above, the "behavior" required begins with "attack." If you were in the army, in a unit that actually "attacks" an enemy, you might know exactly what your troops are supposed to do to accomplish this "attack." Or at least you might think you know. In a unit that has trained together to "attack," then the set of behaviors might even be a common understanding. But behavior is the observable action. What does it look like to "attack?"

In working with teams of people, I've asked them what behaviors they want from their people to meet the challenges of the future. Examine the list they assembled below. Which of these things is truly observable, and therefore measureable?

- Ownership
- Leadership (ask vs. tell)
- Support core values
- Share ideas

- Accountable to the process
- Leadership alignment
- Think
- Accountable
- Provide empowerment
- Share knowledge
- Engage
- Solution finders
- Trust
- Rethink, relook
- Solve problems
- Challenge the status quo
- Accepting ownership
- Dedicated
- Acting with respect toward each other
- Seek out change
- Thinking how to improve
- Listening
- Awareness
- Report problems
- Observing
- Constantly seeking learning
- Work in a disciplined manner
- Follow procedure

On the surface, we all have something that comes to mind with each word or phrase on the list. Chances are, though, that what you think will be different from what I think. So if we are going to develop skills in our workforce and particularly in our leaders, we need concrete and measureable operational descriptions of the specific actions that we want to SEE as our people accomplish their mission in pursuit of our vision. To get those, we have to learn how to talk to each other.

RIGOROUS LEARNING

With the number of those listed behaviors hinting toward problem solving, it's safe to say that if we want to be able to thrive in a future of complexity, scarcity, and fierce competition, we have to cultivate behaviors for learning. Because of the need for very skilled learners among our workforce, the training and education for these outcomes must be rigorous, and embedded into the work we have our people do. Rigor in our learning requires well-defined processes that are strictly enforced and very thorough. Learning embedded in the work allows people to solve problems as they perform their functions in support of the workplace mission, rather than thinking that learning is an outcome of training and education alone. The work is the greatest teacher.

> ## The Work is the Greatest Teacher

While those everyday tasks and behaviors—by leaders and employees alike—must be focused to achieve the mission, it's important to remember that they flow from the organization's values, whether or not those values have been formally stated. Values, good or bad, drive all types of behavior. But that is a discussion for the next chapter. We'll break down levels of learning and discuss behavior changes as a result of that learning in the next chapter, then go beyond that to reaching levels of mastery in Chapter 4, then offer a more concrete rigorous learning system you can use to cultivate behavior for learning in Chapter 9.

CHAPTER SUMMARY

The vision of a workplace has two purposes:

1. Motivating people by creating a common goal
2. Giving people hope

Metavision is seeing the connections within an entity and understanding the impact these connections have on each other. Metavision reveals the potential of the workplace.

The vision tells a story—a story that sets a direction for the future. Like the commander's intent in a military OPORD, vision spells out where we want to be when we're done.

The mission tells the world what the workplace does every day to achieve its vision. Mission is very specific: who, what, when, where, and why. "How" is guided by the workplace's values.

A vision that works focuses not on what the workplace is now but on what it wants to become, so don't base your vision on your current products or market share; base it on the type of workplace you want to become.

The mission describes the actions (therefore the behaviors) required to achieve the vision. We have to articulate the behaviors we want in our leaders and team members, and then develop means to teach and reinforce these correct behaviors.

3

Behavior

What makes people do what they do? Success for businesses, hospitals, schools/universities, churches, government agencies, nonprofits, and for their leaders depends on people behaving in a way that accomplishes the mission of an organization and takes it closer to its vision. In other words, what people do at work must serve the purpose of the company. In order to build a culture that drives continuous improvement, however, workers must also feel that their actions serve a meaningful purpose.

Building the culture of a workplace is a tall order. In every workplace, a culture already exists. This is the way people do things in that workplace, and the practice has been years in the making. To change the culture would mean isolating the good behaviors we want to keep from the bad behaviors we don't, and building systems to help us reinforce those good behaviors. But behavior is tricky. People are complex creatures who do things for all kinds of reasons. Some reasons are apparent; others remain a mystery.

What we know is that the actions people take are generally aligned with their belief systems and the values associated with those beliefs, even when they are acting in response to others. Beliefs and values are shaped over a lifetime, and they have proven to be remarkably resilient. Given the right kind of attention, however, they can change. This is why it's important to create a working environment that attracts the right kind of talent and encourages our employees to do the things we need them to do. One might argue that most employees already do the things we need them to do. After all, most people are pretty compliant at work. They show up on time, try to stay out of trouble, and go home at the end of the day. But compliant workers will never put your workplace on the map. In today's global environment, we need workers who are more than compliant. We need workers who are engaged. When we succeed in making the transition from compliant workers to engaged workers, everyone benefits.

FROM COMPLIANCE TO ENGAGEMENT

Employee engagement has been a hot topic for years. Companies view engaged workers as a competitive advantage, but getting people engaged at work doesn't happen spontaneously. Here's a roadmap you can follow to build an engaged workforce over time.

Most workplaces exist within a culture of compliance. People either don't expect their individual needs to be met on the job (other than their need for a paycheck), or they've never realized how meaningful a good job can be. It shouldn't be surprising then that it takes significant effort for a leader to turn compliant employees into engaged team members. This can't be done in one big step. It's like the long journey that begins with a single step. That first step is to get them *involved*.

In most cases, all you need to do to get compliant workers involved is to ask. Because they're already at work and want to stay out of trouble, they'll usually agree, for example, to serve on a project team when asked. A note of caution so you'll be fully prepared; a culture of involvement usually begins with the newly involved employee's most common contribution, complaining, so don't expect too much.

"They never listen to anyone around here."
"I told them about that problem years ago and they just don't care."
"This place used to care about people, but now it's all about money."

Sound familiar? You asked, and they told you, and if you do the same thing as previous leaders have done—offer platitudes, ignore feedback, and continue with business as usual—they'll still be complaining when you leave for greener pastures. If you want different results, you have to listen—really listen—to what's being said, address the complaints of the speakers and those underlying issues, and continue to share your vision. You don't have to give them whatever they ask for, but you need to discuss their needs, listen carefully to their input (even if it's only complaints), and do what you can to reassure them that their input matters.

When you apply some of your people's ideas and input, keeping them involved in their actual implementation, you'll begin to shape a culture of enthusiasm. Few things fire people up like seeing one of their ideas work; it's the same feeling as winning a game. People who move from involvement to enthusiasm are people who see a clear gain from their participation. Allow them to participate in something like a weeklong improvement event. At the end of that week, you'll be able to see who is moved by the results and who isn't. Enthusiasm typically brings more ideas and more willingness to try things, but you're likely to hear comments such as "This week was fantastic! We love kaizen events! I can't wait until the kaizen team comes back and we can do this again!" Sure, such comments sound great, and those that make them are clearly enthusiastic. But they're still not engaged.

Leadersights: Learning

One way to get people to participate is to pull them together as a problem-solving team, focused on a single problem that they get to pick, analyze, and solve with the help of a facilitator to guide them through a defined process. Put four or five people together from a few different sections of your workplace. Give them a couple of hours every week to work together (this might be for 6 or more weeks). Have the facilitator lead them through activities to find a good, relatively small-scope problem that affects all of the participants, then break that problem down to its root cause and develop five or six different ways to solve the problem. Have the team test these different solutions in small experiments to find out which one gets the very best result, then implement that best way throughout the workplace. Post the team's weekly activity in an area where everyone can see the progress they are making and share other employee insights as well.

The single characteristic that distinguishes a culture of engagement from one of enthusiasm is self-direction. Engaged people make improvements to their work on their own initiative and then come looking for you to share what they've done. Imagine the progress that a workplace could make if everyone were making small improvements to their work area and trying new things every day. Of course, without some consistency and control mechanism, this could get chaotic pretty quickly, so I've worked out a way to allow leaders to have some sense of control while empowering people to act. See Chapter 9!

What it boils down to is this: How much effort is an individual willing to expend to succeed at work? In the culture of compliance, people offer the minimum effort required to stay out of trouble. This does not mean to imply these individuals are slackers. Depending on the nature of the work, even this level of effort can be significant. As the culture matures through involvement, enthusiasm, and then engagement, they apply increasing levels of discretionary effort to their work, leaving the concept of "doing the minimum" behind.

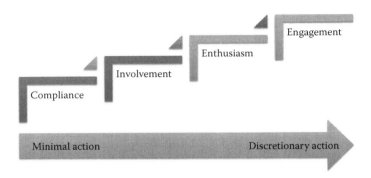

If we're going to cultivate a culture of continuous improvement, people have to do more than the minimum; people have to be engaged. It is up to leaders to design work that makes doing more an attractive option, and it shouldn't have anything to do with money. People devote their effort more readily to activities that offer them meaningfulness. This is why some people who are merely compliant at work are also tremendous contributors in their churches or community organizations. They may coach Little League or volunteer at a homeless shelter. To tap into this human capacity on the job as well (we still want them to volunteer in the community), we need to make the work more meaningful. In other words, we need to give people a good reason to become engaged. The best way to begin is with clear expectations.

SETTING EXPECTATIONS

How do we tell people what we expect them to do at work? Most workplaces have fairly detailed job descriptions or standard operating procedures (SOPs) that define the responsibilities of a position and may include a very specific task list. Some workplaces have standardized work for all positions that details each of the steps required to do the work, as well as how to do the work and how much time it should take. Even in these highly specified instances, however, there are core behaviors we expect from people that aren't typically communicated, neither verbally nor in writing. These include showing up on time, in proper work attire, at the right place, perhaps properly punched in, with the right equipment, well rested and fed, and maybe even being nice to coworkers. If we don't tell people what we expect them to do, they won't do what we expect of them. Is it surprising we often end up disappointed or angry with workers for not doing what we didn't tell them to do?

> **If we don't tell people what we expect them to do, they won't do what we expect**

In previous chapters, we discussed how a leader's mindset is shaped by understanding value from the customer's perspective, translating that value into a vision of the future for the organization, and then spelling out a mission to guide what people do every day. This combination of mission and vision sets a goal. One purpose of the goal is to drive positive behavior, but in pursuit of this goal, the potential to drive bad behavior is always there. Tyco, Enron, and Lehman Brothers, to name just a few, are glaring examples of corporate behavioral meltdowns. The causes of such failures are complex, but if we examined each in detail we'd more than likely find a common thread: inappropriate behavior, spurred by overzealous pursuit of rewards for achieving stated or unstated goals.

To build a dynamically stable workplace, everyone needs to know that there is a right and a wrong way to behave; the ones we highlight in our values.

ORGANIZATIONAL VALUES

Defining the company's values is important. Values tell everyone what behaviors the company expects of its employees, but if no mechanism exists to enforce these "right" behaviors, the organization will never achieve its true potential.

Many organizations publish their core values for all to see. For example, LINAK US Inc., a manufacturer of electric linear actuator systems, posts their values on their website. Here's what they say:

Our Values

The results LINAK has achieved through the years are based on a set of values, which define what we stand for. We place great importance on our values and we take steps to measure how well we live up to them.

- Customer orientation
  - Listening to and understanding our customers' needs are the key to developing truly innovative solutions. Wherever our customers are, LINAK wants to be. Our subsidiaries understand the local culture, speak the language, and are close to the customers in order to serve them in the best possible way.
- Creativity
  - Creative thinking is how LINAK got started in the first place. Creativity goes hand in hand with innovation—both when it comes to developing new solutions and finding new applications for our products. As long as creative ideas result in added value to our customers, LINAK will pursue them unremittingly.
- The will to change
  - We live in a rapidly changing world. LINAK has committed itself to always be at the cutting edge of the market. In order to continuously improve and deliver innovative solutions we always stay flexible and open to new challenges and opportunities.
- Loyalty, openness, and honesty
  - We are loyal toward our values and we are loyal toward our customers. Confidential information stays confidential at LINAK.
  - We associate with each other and with our customers openly and honestly. We are open and honest in all matters pertaining [to] our daily work at LINAK. We discuss the problems we face openly in order to seek better solutions.
- Enthusiasm and individual efficiency
  - Our culture is based on enthusiastic employees always seeking to make a difference for the customer, for the company and for themselves. This includes a dedication to efficiency by using LEAN in most possible processes in connection with our daily work.
- Job satisfaction and helpfulness
  - LINAK strives for all employees to be satisfied with and proud of the results we achieve. Employees seek and expect influence

on their daily work. We take an active interest in the well-being of each other at LINAK. We help, support, and encourage each other to reach new heights.

LINAK displays an abbreviated form of these values on banners throughout their facility (see Figure 3.1).

Skretting Australia, the fish feed manufacturer mentioned briefly in the previous chapter, spent a long time carefully deciding what values it wanted to share with the workforce (and the rest of the world). This company built an exceptional framework of behaviors tied to key performance indicators (safety, quality, communication, teamwork, and accountability) and linked them back to four core values (reliable, open, competent, and innovative). Figure 3.2 shows a matrix of how these core values and key performance indicators intersect.

Both LINAK and Skretting Australia have tied performance appraisals for their leaders to company values, but the application of these values goes way beyond once-a-year feedback. Leaders apply them every day, intervening when necessary to keep good behaviors on track and snuff out bad behaviors—an example of coaching (and accountability) at its best.

The three components of an organization's operating philosophy (vision, mission, and values) set behavioral expectations that forge a vital link to worker satisfaction. In Chapter 1, we talked about "awareness" as one of three primary contributors to satisfaction. The more workers are

FIGURE 3.1
LINAK values.

Living the values

Reliable   Open   Competent   Innovative

Skretting Australia

	High performance	Expected performance	Low performance
Safety	Delivers safety improvements company wide and ensures our obligations to the environment and community are met. Safety first. Promotes safety and acts upon the safety concerns of others Adheres to safety standards and proactively identifies safety risks Seeks and delivers best practice in safety	Recognises and raises safety improvements Recognises the safety concerns of colleagues Identifies safety risks Accepts the current safety rules and systems	Lacks awareness about company safety Dismisses the safety concerns of colleagues Unaware of safety risks and standards Negative toward safety rules and systems
Quality	Looks for quality opportunities and fixes quality issues to ensure our obligations to the environment and community are met Always seeking quality improvement opportunities and supports others with improvements Acts upon the quality needs of internal and external customers Drives continuous improvement in quality	Knows and follows quality systems and standards Recognises the quality concerns of colleagues Aware of the quality concerns of internal and external customers Accepts the current quality systems and standards	Rarely raises quality issues or opportunities Dismisses the quality concerns of colleagues Fails to recognise the quality needs of internal and external customers Negative toward quality systems and standards
Communication	Communicates ahead of time and improves communication channels Communicates with transparency, honesty, and maintains respect for others Communicates confidently and ensures colleagues act upon instructions Actively engages with others to seek creative solutions	Communicates on time with a predictable demeanour and maintains established communication channels Communicates to colleagues with honesty Communicates effectively so that messages are thoroughly understood Freely offers knowledge during communication	Offers information late and uses inconsistent communication channels Communicates errors and/or speaks negatively to others Does not ensure instructions are thoroughly understood Does not share important facts and avoids talking about system and people improvements
Teamwork	Respects others and maintains a positive role in the team Actively supports change and provides valuable ideas to deliver solutions between teams. Goes out of way to support team Leads by example and supports others to follow all company policies Welcomes further training and is willing to take on more responsibility	Maintains a good attitude and is a team player Brings new ideas to the team and suggests solutions between teams Follows all company policies Prepared to learn and maintains current responsibilities	Blames others and argues with team members Does not offer new ideas and does not support activity between teams Needs to be reminded to follow all company policies Not willing to develop and avoids responsibility
Accountability	Recognises the needs of others and ensures tasks are completed ahead of time Speaks out with good intent and willing to coach colleagues in their responsibilities Improves systems so errors are not repeated Acknowledges the issues and works to resolve the root cause of problems	Willing to share the load and complete tasks on time Willing to speak to colleagues when they are not maintaining their responsibilities Accepts responsibility and resolves the implication of an error Willing to assist in the resolution of the root cause of problems	Does not assist others and does not complete tasks Only concerned with personal responsibilities Leaves it to others to discover an error or clean up Accepts repeating problems

FIGURE 3.2
Skretting behaviors.

aware—the more they know about what others expect of them and about whether or not they are meeting those expectations—the more engaged they are likely to become. And if they are meeting or exceeding expectations more often than not, they're far more likely to be satisfied employees.

The results of employee surveys, no matter the organization or the leader, usually list the top complaint of employees as either "communication" or "lack of communication." Such complaints, of course, are directed squarely at leaders. True, leaders must communicate effectively, but even if they were "perfect" communicators, they often have only imperfect information to communicate. These information gaps cause problems, especially in environments where trust is already weak.

Information provided by leaders, or company values displayed on banners or posters, are laudable attempts to communicate a company's expectations. None of this effort means much, however, unless a climate of trust exists between leaders and those they lead. **Effective communication is a function of trust**. In almost every case, how effectively a message is transmitted or received is far more dependent on the trust factor than on the content or medium of the communiqué. We discussed trust briefly in earlier chapters, but it is such a pivotal leadersights concept I want to reexamine it here.

TRUST

When there is strong trust between the person delivering a message and those receiving it, recipients are usually willing to ask about any perceived information gaps. Leaders in workplaces who are willing to open a dialogue show they have workers' best interests at heart and are behaving in a way that will serve everyone's needs. Gaps in information are acknowledged simply as things "we don't know right now."

Where trust is weak—a far too common reality since we have a few hundred years' experience of breaking trust between leaders and the led—the workforce often interprets these information gaps as the deliberate withholding of facts, if not outright deception. Such false perceptions can result in the spread of rumors that are more destructive than helpful. They can also create factions among employees that sever existing collaborative ties. Often these fissures go unresolved for years until something happens that is so traumatic it forces everyone to recognize that their survival depends on helping each other out.

Great workplaces are built on trust, and the most fundamental goal of leadership is to build that trust.

Building Trust

I frequently speak to groups that are bombarded with demands to "build trust." It's not that these folks don't recognize how important building trust is to success, it's that no one ever tells them how to do it. What actually builds trust? How are they supposed to behave? To answer these questions, we only have to look at our own life experiences. We all know that when you're caught lying to a friend or spouse, it is very hard to restore trust between you, thus the advice of our friends and family; "don't lie." In statements of company values, "don't lie" is conveyed through terms like "honesty," "integrity," and "reliability."

If we ask couples who have been together for years what causes most of the disagreements in their relationship, we learn that one didn't do something the other expected of them (or vice versa). The result is always the same; trust was broken. It doesn't matter that the expectation was never spoken (one of those "you-should-have-known" things). Of course, we can't act on what we don't know, either in our personal lives or at work. This is why each party must seek to understand and shape the true expectations of the other, and each must work to satisfy the expectations of the other. Trust is a two-way street.

Leadersights: Learning, Loving, and Letting Go

To build and maintain trust in the workplace (which is far more difficult than doing so in more intimate relationships) focus on the two key components discussed earlier: clear expectations and vulnerability. Be diligent in articulating your expectations of your employees and listen carefully to the expectations your employees have of you, allowing this flow of expectations to operate in both directions. Discuss these openly so that everyone is crystal clear on what the expectations are and everyone agrees they are reasonable and achievable.

The only way this bidirectional flow can work is if leaders are willing to be vulnerable. The party in a position of power must take steps to subject himself, his reputation, and his livelihood to the performance of the other party in a way that's apparent.

Inevitably, some projects fail. Sometimes organizations lose money, or make decisions that generate bad press or fail to meet goals. Sometimes people let us down. If the leader (the party in a position of power) always reacts harshly to failure—an all-too-common occurrence in business—the result will be a culture of blame and fear, where trust is thoroughly broken. Under such circumstances most workers remain compliant, for fear of losing their jobs if nothing else, but few if any are likely to become engaged.

Life is not perfect, but leaders can't let this prevent them from continuing to develop people and giving them other opportunities to succeed. After every failure, it's important to spend time to jointly discover the true causes of the failure and then to jointly develop and enact countermeasures to prevent these causes from negatively affecting future efforts. Giving people another chance to benefit from what they've just learned is a trust-builder. It's also the engine of the learning organization.

LISTENING

As mentioned earlier, communicating expectations and building trust are critical factors in developing and maintaining an engaged workforce. They're also two-sided propositions. Leaders who will not listen to their people build one of the biggest barriers to a relationship based on trust. Of course, no leader would actually admit he or she doesn't listen, but I've seen such people in every type of workplace, at all levels, and they are universally destructive.

Listening is not a passive activity. It takes time and it requires action. To listen well is hard work, especially when we already have streams of information and thought running through our minds. It is no wonder people accuse leaders of never listening. They're often surrounded by so many important, urgent, and/or crisis-driven items (not to mention the noise of everyday life) that it's hard to be able to stop, focus, and understand what someone is saying, and then jump right back into the fray. Nevertheless, for those who wish to create great workplaces, listening is a game-changer.

Listening is a loving action. To listen effectively, we have to stop what we are doing and give our full attention to the speaker. This is usually reserved for those we care about most. Listening puts their needs above our needs. If we don't, we risk frustrating them, losing their respect, or forcing them to disengage with us and seek another person with whom to share.

Think about it. When a leader (whom everyone knows is constantly busy solving issues around the workplace) stops and carefully listens, he or she is investing precious and limited time in the speaker. Most of us have experienced the other end of this, frustrated at a boss who won't make time to talk us for even a few minutes. Conversely, when a leader actively listens, he or she sends a message to the speaker that says "You're so significant to me that I'm setting everything else aside to spend time with you." With our fast-paced lives today, we can't afford not to listen to others carefully. In the final analysis, if someone has worked up the courage to share his or her issue with you, understand that there is nothing more important to that person at that moment. To act as if it is unimportant to you reinforces the message that they aren't important at all.

Leadersights: Listening (and Loving)

Build buffers into your workday schedule so you have time to stop and listen. You need not always have an answer to their question or solution for their problem, and that's okay. Initially, just listening may be enough. The relationships established through listening allow leaders to learn more about the values and beliefs that motivate their people. Being able to explain how a change at work supports these values and beliefs makes it easier to get workers engaged and bought-into the change.

In Chapter 8, we'll talk more about the role and importance of scheduled "listening time" when developing standardized work.

Listening is also a learning function because it is instrumental—both individually and collectively—in advancing learning. The success of workplaces in the future will be dependent on the ability of people to learn what they need to know faster than their competitors. In lean systems, effective leaders know developing that ability in their people is their primary job.

BEHAVIOR FOR LEARNING

People (and by extension, workplaces) learn in four domains: psychomotor, cognitive, affective, and social. The first three domains each consist of a series of learning levels, with each level resulting in greater insight and expertise. As people go about their daily lives, learning happens concurrently in all domains. To create a great workplace that becomes a true learning organization, leaders need to develop specific strategies for bringing people to the highest levels of learning in each domain.

Psychomotor Learning

This domain describes how people learn new physical skills. It deals with actual performance—how we do things and how we get better at them. We progress through several distinct levels as we hone our psychomotor skills, from simple perception (reflexive actions), through guided responses (deliberate, thought-driven action), to autonomic abilities (action that requires no distinct thinking). Learning to drive a car provides the simplest and clearest example of this concept. The first time behind the wheel, new drivers mentally run through all the steps they need to remember, but over time they operate a car with no deliberate thought (granted, with varying levels of proficiency).

As we repeat the steps of any physical process, we improve our skills until we become experts, potentially becoming creators in our own right.

When we talk about teaching someone how to do a job, we're also talking about the psychomotor domain. The concept of standardized work relies heavily on psychomotor skills, since it requires that everyone do the work the same way each time (see Chapter 8). Standardized work becomes the training tool, and we have to get perfect quality from every team member doing that job.

Leadersights: Learning

Clearly define processes and require that everyone who does that work do it the same way every time. Enforce this rigorously to build new habits and improve skills.

Cognitive Learning

This domain focuses on how we think about our current situation when solving problems, how our brains function while we're engaged in an experience, and what we're thinking as we go through it. When we're teaching someone how to think about doing his or her job (bring your brain to work), we're talking about the cognitive domain. In a lean environment, this domain is critical, since we want team members to know how to solve the problems they are likely to encounter with their work.

There are six levels of learning in the cognitive domain: knowing, understanding, applying, analyzing, creating, and evaluating. The first three are fairly linear in progression. We learn new, basic facts about something (remembering); we gain more comprehension as we interact with others or the work (understanding); and finally, we reach a point where we can apply what we've learned in a specific situation (applying). Most training programs for new hires are structured around these three levels of learning.

The three higher levels of learning—analyzing, creating, and evaluating—are referred to collectively as problem-solving levels and seem to be nonlinear.

Humans are hardwired to solve problems—after all, we've managed to survive and thrive for quite some time now—but to take advantage of these innate instincts at work, we need to offer people very specific education, training, and development in the three higher levels as follows:

- *Analyzing.* Breaking down a particular problem to identify the contributing factors and their influence on the whole issue
- *Creating.* Synthesizing alternative methods to achieve the outcomes associated with the problem
- *Evaluating.* Judging whether one alternative is better or worse than another

We build brainpower in our employees by focusing on these three levels and can do so by taking advantage of the natural curiosity and problem-solving capability people bring to work every day. These levels are not linear and progressive; rather, they swirl around one another, influencing the information available and our interpretation of that information.

For example, as we seek to understand the contribution of one piece of a process we may be analyzing, we bring our experience to the mix and evaluate its relevance to the current need. While keeping our initial analysis in mind, we then create and discard various potential solutions to a problem. These potential solutions may provide additional information to help us more clearly define the problem and/or may point us to other information sources to further our analysis. As we experiment or go through trial-and-error iterations with our solutions, each instance produces more information and further refines our catalog of things to try.

Leadersights: Learning

For every problem encountered in the workplace, coach people through the critical thinking steps required to analyze the problem, develop a solution, and evaluate that solution. (Chapter 9 outlines simple ways to teach these cognitive skills through the use of a rigorous learning system.)

Affective Learning

The affective domain relates specifically to how people feel about what they're learning, or how they connect with a concept emotionally. This connection, which applies to both teacher (leader) and student (the led), is what comes into play when leaders are trying to get people to take ownership of changes in the workplace. The more valuable a subject is to the person, the more energy he or she will expend to listen, understand, apply, organize, evaluate, and synthesize the content of the message and the environment in which it is presented. And the more people there are who recognize the value of what they are being taught, the more likely they'll be to take an active role in implementing new solutions.

The affective learning domain consists of five levels: receiving, responding, valuing, organizing, and characterizing. These levels represent the span of emotional connection to learning something new. At the lower levels, we have little emotional investment in receiving and/or responding. As we discover more, and connect these discoveries to things we learned in the past, increasing its relevance, we place greater value on the new information (valuing). As the value of new information increases, we categorize this material in a way that allows us to access it rapidly (organizing). As we access the new information again and again, we begin to behave differently, incorporating what we've learned into our daily behavior and our character (characterizing).

The affective learning process is fundamental to creating new habits. We can't simply tell people they need to do this or that and expect them to go and do it. If it is inconsistent with their existing beliefs and values, they will discard it as soon as they hear it. They will comply if we force the issue, but only with the minimum effort required to stay out of trouble, potentially reverting to the old way whenever they can.

Leadersights: Loving

Take time to explain why people need to know, understand, and apply what you are teaching them. Draw connections to past successes. The more compelling your argument, the more energy people will devote to learning.

During World War II, the War Manpower Commission developed the Training within Industry (TWI) service to ensure supervisors in factories that produced war materiel were able to train new hires—many who had never done this kind of work before—to be effective very quickly. Three components of the TWI approach included job instruction, job methods, and job relations.

While predating the publication of Bloom's Taxonomy of psychomotor, cognitive, and affective domains, TWI strategies employed a similar approach to reach the highest levels of learning described in each domain. They also provided very specific, even scripted, sessions for developing job skills. After the war, the United States furnished TWI documents to Japanese companies in order to help them achieve a speedier recovery during reconstruction. As Japanese firms applied these principles, they laid the foundation for companies such as Toyota to become lean organizations in the future. (TWI documents continue to be available, free of charge, from a variety of sources on the Internet.)

Social Learning

The social domain is a fourth dimension of learning. This domain deals with relationships between individuals, with relationships between people and the workplace, and with relationships between what people are thinking and what they're actually doing in the workplace. Changes to the ways in which we work, the ways we supervise, and the ways we reorganize the workplace often fall into the social domain.

In a nutshell, social learning refers to the ways in which people learn by observing others in different environments. When we watch people do something in a particular setting, we observe the consequences of their actions. Should we get a chance to try the same task, we call on these observations to decide whether we want to reproduce (or avoid) the same effect. This method of observing cause and effect is how people learn from very early childhood, and it continues to be a powerful learning strategy throughout life, both on and off the job.

Most companies put a lot of effort into screening applicants and hiring the person who they believe has the best aptitude for the job in question. Then, they move on to job instruction in earnest. Once this period of qualification is finished, they typically treat the employee as if his or her learning is over. In reality, it has only just begun.

> **Structure the workplace to allow workers to observe each other as they work.**

When groups of people perform the same, or similar, work, some develop expertise faster than others. These experts often find it very difficult to explain how they do the job differently to get a smoother, faster, and better result. If we structure the workplace to allow workers to observe each other as they work, we increase the chance that they will detect the subtle differences in how each performs and incorporate those as improvements into their own work routines. Then, once these new work routines are identified, we need to document them as "knack points" to teach others in the future.

Leadersights: Letting Go

To benefit from social learning, organize the workforce into small teams of four or five people and assign a coach to each team. The work assigned should dictate the number of people on the team, and together, the team should be able to deliver a product or service complete to a customer. In other words, the team should be responsible for some whole piece of work, be it a subassembly, a report, or a meal. Arrange their work space so they can easily interact with each other and see how others approach their tasks. Ideally, you will be able to rotate the team members through the different work spaces so they will have different responsibilities in each, learning and developing multiple skills as they do. For a lot more on teams, see Chapter 5.

Examples

Here are two examples that summarize how the different learning domains come into play when performing a task. Your assignment is to develop an example for your workplace and send it to me.

Fishing:

- Casting and reeling are psychomotor skills.
- Selecting fishing holes, selecting bait or lures, and fishing at a particular depth are cognitive skills.
- The feeling we experience when we have that big fish on the hook both reinforces our decision to go fishing and makes us want to do it again. This is the affective domain.
- Watching how your buddies fight a fish to bring it in, sharing stories about the one that got away, and deciding when to move to a new spot as a result of some change in the environment all fall into the social domain, which overlaps all the others.

Golf:

- Perfecting your swing is a psychomotor skill.
- Selecting which club to use, adjusting your swing based on the lie of the ball, and reading the green for a putt are cognitive skills.
- Dealing with the emotions of golf falls into the affective domain (and golf always seems to mess with our emotions). It's hard to beat the feeling of hitting a huge drive off the tee or sinking a ten-foot putt, but golf is a difficult and often frustrating sport. Maybe it is just being away from work or from projects at home that makes us value our golf experiences, rather than the game itself!
- Watching your buddies try new clubs or techniques, discussing the round in the clubhouse, posting handicaps, and watching Gary Player training videos are parts of the social domain.

Changing Our Behavior

It seems reasonable that before leaders go trying to change the behavior of their people, they should be able to manage changes in their own behavior first. Anyone who has ever tried to lose weight, quit smoking, or stop drinking alcohol knows how challenging changing habits can be. I'm not a therapist, so I'm just going to share my observations in an effort to provide some food for thought for you leaders and potential leaders regarding your behavior.

I recently lost 30 pounds over 9 months by setting a daily calorie target and keeping track of everything I ate, trying desperately to stay under the target. I also started exercising, initially because when I exercised I could eat more! I had an app on my smartphone that made keeping track pretty easy. When I finally decided that the gut had to go, I used that app and focused on accuracy of the data input. For everything I wanted to eat, I checked its caloric content first, often asking restaurant wait staff for the nutritional information of their menu items. I really became quite obsessive–compulsive about it. I focused ONLY on calories. When I exercised, I earned extra calories, so I could eat more. That focus made it simple to follow and I could eat whatever I wanted as long as I came in under the target at the end of the day. My goal weight was 180 pounds (after starting at 221). Following this process of tracking the details of my consumption and exercise, I lost about 2 pounds per week. The plan was to switch then to maintenance mode where I could keep the weight off. When I hit 186, I rewarded myself with a trip to Hawaii to walk the Maui Oceanfront Half-Marathon with my wife. I was running for the first time in years without my knees killing me; I felt great.

I felt so great I convinced myself that I had learned enough over those months that I could mentally keep track of everything without having to obsessively track them using my app. I knew that to maintain the weight instead of losing weight, I could eat more every day. So, I stopped fanatically logging everything. I started a new job that required me to learn a bunch of new rules and create a bunch of new course materials. We moved from Kentucky to Ohio over a drawn-out 6 months and involved moving into an apartment first, then buying a house, then selling the Kentucky house that had been home for 12 years. My three kids deployed with the Navy, moved to Maryland, and started college all within weeks of each other. We experienced a brutal and lonely winter in our new home.

You know how this turns out…The next thing I know, I stand on the scale and top 210 again. Fortunately, I'm exercising again (hopefully not just for the short term) and I'm watching what I eat and tracking occasionally, but probably not carefully enough to drive myself to my goal weight any time soon. My app still reminds me three times a day to log what I've eaten. So what did I learn about changing my own behavior?

1. I made a distinct and clear decision that I had to change or there would be serious health consequences.
2. I set an aggressive goal, one I knew would be very difficult to achieve, but not impossible.
3. I created an accountability structure; logging my weight, my exercise, and my food intake into the app (by the way, the app is called LoseIt! It was a free download and fully functional).
4. It took rigid discipline to check all those food labels, search the web for fast food nutrition information, and log everything. Even when I would grab a peppermint from the jar I made a point to stop and log it.
5. As soon as I turned away from my accountability structure and relaxed the discipline, I backslid. It is significantly harder for me to get back into the swing of logging everything because I know if I do, I'll have to stay in it.

So, what do my personal weight-loss lessons have to do with you changing your working behavior? A lot, I think. And as I've learned more about human behavior, as unpredictable as it can be, I think we have a lot more control over behavior than many people would like to think. We do need some structure though, and we need a deliberate plan if we are going to make changes to what we do and what our people do with us in our workplaces.

Every behavioral action is preceded by a conscious thought, however, fleeting or solid it may be. Every behavioral action is followed by some consequence that either positively reinforces the action with a reward, or discourages the action with some punishment. The rewards or punishment are often quite subtle. These affect our thoughts in future behavior decisions we make. See Figure 3.3.

FIGURE 3.3
Behavior cycle.

Ideally, we would begin to change our behavior with a change in the way we think. Changing the way we think is extremely difficult. Our thinking goes back to those beliefs and values we have shaped over a lifetime. Knowing the facts about the consequences of our behavioral choices is rarely sufficient to drive the new actions needed. Alan Deutschman illustrates this beautifully in his book "Change or Die" (Harper Business, 2007). In it, he describes three cases (heart disease patients, convicted criminals, and unionized autoworkers) where changing behavior is required and provides statistics for how difficult it is to do.

In the case of heart disease patients, he discusses how diet, lifestyle, smoking, and stress have been known contributors to heart disease for decades, yet millions of people are still overweight, sedentary, smoke, and stress-out every day of their lives. We know these things and we tell ourselves everyday "one of these days, I have to quit." It is simply too difficult to put down the cigarette and go for a walk, as simple as the advice sounds.

In other cases, we may not believe that taking a particular action will have a positive effect. Our thoughts may also allow us to rationalize our current behavior as acceptable. "All those other people need to change because I'm the only one who works around here." Yes, thinking gets in the way of every change.

For me, the only thoughts I had standing on that scale were that I was sick of looking down at a big belly and sick of being winded after climbing a flight of stairs. I had run the Air Force Marathon in 1999, so I know how it feels to be in great physical shape. I know how it feels, but I still didn't have to actually DO anything. I've had those thoughts a hundred times without doing anything about it. The key difference this time was that I had decided to take some action, made a plan, and then immediately put that plan into action. How many times before have I promised myself that I'd start exercising or dieting on Monday, only to have Monday come and go with another candy bar on my lips? That morning, I went out and exercised for the first time in a couple of years. That morning, I downloaded the app that a friend told me about and started keeping track. The only other thing I wish I had done then was to enlist a few other people to go with me. They could have helped to keep me accountable to my daily goal. Without a supporting group, the challenge is more difficult, but still not impossible if you can muster the will and the discipline yourself. My caution here is that even when you can do it yourself, as soon as you look away, you'll backslide, so having a support group will help.

In "Change or Die," Deutschman finds common ground in changes made in his three case studies that he summarizes as "Relate, Repeat, Reframe." The group I wish I had assembled would satisfy the relate requirement. Having a supporting relationship has a powerful impact on people. Abraham Maslow wrote about this in 1943 in an article entitled "A dynamic theory of human motivation." He found that people have a compelling need to love and affiliate with each other. He worked this into his Hierarchy of Needs that most of us learn about in a college psychology or business class discussion about motivating people. I'll talk a little more about motivation in the next chapter, so for now let's refocus on behavior.

To make a change in your workplace culture, you will need to change the way most people think. We've already established that this is a tall order, but not impossible. It has to begin with one leader (YOU) deciding to change what you do in an effort to get a better performance result. So, set a goal about what you want to become—and challenge yourself in doing so. Make it difficult but not impossible. Then build a support group from your people. Organize them into small teams and assign everyone the responsibility of holding each other accountable to working toward the new goal.

Next, build an accountability system to make your goal and your progress toward that goal clear and obvious to everyone. We'll describe this in detail in Chapter 7 when we discuss visual management systems. Ask your support group to help you find better ways to work toward the goal and post that progress as well. We'll integrate this discussion in Chapter 9 when we discuss rigorous learning systems. Chapters 7 through 9 provide physical structures for you to drive new behaviors and thinking, and that new thinking is what Deutschman calls "reframe." It's what I call our only hope for the future, where the global marketplace and global constraints will force us to find new ways to succeed.

CHAPTER SUMMARY

The roadmap for behavior at work typically follows this path:
Compliance–Involvement–Enthusiasm–Engagement

- Don't expect to make the leap from "compliance" to "engagement" in a single bound.

- Set clear performance and behavior expectations and reinforce them every day.
  - Expectations begin with the vision and mission of an organization. The vision and mission dictate the company's values. No matter how carefully constructed, however, values are meaningless if there is no plan to hold people accountable to them.
- Communicating expectations is a two-way street that requires leaders to place renewed emphasis on their own listening skills.
  - Effective communication is a function of trust.
  - Building trust requires clear expectations from each party, with both working to satisfy those expectations.
  - Building trust also requires the leader to make him or herself vulnerable to the performance of the team.
- Listening is critical for learning.
- Learning occurs in four domains, concurrently, every day:
  - Psychomotor skills get work done
  - Cognitive skills let people make improvements and solve problems
  - Affective learning makes the work worth doing
  - Social learning makes the other three possible
- Changing behavior is difficult but not impossible
  - Begin with a goal (challenge)
  - Build a support group (your team to hold you accountable)
  - Build an accountability structure (standardized work)
  - Stick to it with discipline (repetition)
  - Reward yourself, but don't stop keeping track!

4

Self-Efficacy and the Continuous Improvement Engine

Flowing from the research in social learning and behavior is a concept called self-efficacy. In the introduction, I mentioned self-efficacy as arguably the most important foundational component for enabling a culture of continuous improvement. Self-efficacy is the level of confidence a person feels about his or her ability to do a particular task. Unlike self-confidence or self-esteem however, which are more generic feelings of confidence and worth, self-efficacy is task-specific, which makes it particularly relevant for workplaces and for leaders.

Self-efficacy provides the bridge between any change initiative and the work. See whether this metaphor helps: in a smartphone, we have hardware and apps. Lying between these two layers is the operating system that allows the apps to activate the hardware to accomplish what the user intends. If the hardware represents the work we do, and the apps represent all the initiatives we have launched over the years to try to make changes in the workplace, then self-efficacy acts as the operating system. Self-efficacy allows people to take the information and structure from the change initiatives (the apps) and embed them into the work we do (the hardware) to get the results we need to satisfy demanding customers. Without individual willingness and capability to take what the initiative teaches and apply it to their work, those initiatives, regardless of the volume of training and activity, will fail.

Leaders can take relatively simple, practical steps in the design of work that are highly likely to increase the level of self-efficacy in their employees.

Beside research papers in psychology, the only place I've seen the word "efficacy" in the mainstream is in the fine print of some drug advertisements in magazines. Efficacy in these cases refers to the power the drug has to have an effect on the symptoms it is trying to treat. Higher efficacy means the drug is more effective. Self-efficacy works much the same. Higher self-efficacy means the person is more effective in performing the tasks we assign them at work. In a sense, we could call self-efficacy someone's personal power to have an effect on the workplace.

> **Self-Efficacy = Personal Power to have an effect on the workplace.**

After years of studying and teaching topics related to process improvement, lean, the Toyota Production System, and problem solving, I'm convinced that self-efficacy is the single most important concept for leaders to understand to build a sustainable culture of continuous improvement. If we can get this right, our improvement systems will operate autonomously.

THREE CRITICAL ACTIONS

The reason I believe this is the most important concept for leadership lies in the behaviors associated with high self-efficacy, and how consistent this is with the way people in highly effective workplaces behave. People with high self-efficacy are more likely than others to do three key things:

1. Improve their personal work and workstations without prompting
2. Try new things others might suggest (or accept more risk)
3. Persist after failure

When I described engaged employees in the last chapter, I said "imagine the progress a workplace could make if everyone were making small improvements to their work area and trying new things every day." Add to that the willingness to persist through initial failures until something works better and there is no limit to the progress a workplace could make! Higher self-efficacy bridges the gap between enthusiastic employees and engaged team members.

CONTRIBUTORS TO SELF-EFFICACY

Studies have shown that there are just a few critical contributors to higher self-efficacy. Understanding these critical elements and designing work to promote them will change everything.

Mastery

The main element of self-efficacy is mastery. This reflects a high level of skill, competence, or experience with the task at hand, plus an understanding of the broader system in which we work. Becoming an expert at any skill requires extended hours of practice doing a task the same way every time. This way, with every successful completion of the task, we should get just a little better, and we should feel the small burst of satisfaction that comes with doing a job right (however, subtle that burst may be).

Think about learning to play a new song on a musical instrument. At first, the musician might fumble through the notes as he reads the music and tries to play along properly. Over time, after playing the song the way it is written every time, the musician becomes competent, and the song sounds the way intended. However, expertise goes beyond mere competence. When a talented musician *masters* a song, he will typically change it slightly when he plays it, making it his own, while preserving the original melody so the song is still recognizable, but personalized.

At work, the sheet music is the standardized work developed for the specific workstation or position (see Chapter 8 for info on standardized work). To turn employees into experts, deliberately and carefully teach them to do the work as designed and require them to follow the standardized work, as written, every time they work. The job instruction piece of Training within Industry (TWI) described in the previous chapter is the most effective way I have seen this occur, provided the trainer executes it properly. As people become experts, they will try new things and discover new ways to do the work that make it easier, faster, or otherwise more efficient. This becomes the cornerstone for a culture of continuous improvement.

I need to emphasize that leaders must require experts for all their working positions. That means the work needs to require a certain level of expertise and not be too simple or repetitive. These jobs need to be redesigned to add complexity without overburdening workers. Redesigning the work is the leader's job. This is not for some anonymous engineering group or manager. This is an intimate responsibility that requires intimate understanding of the capabilities, motivations, and satisfiers for the people doing the work.

Since mass production began, people in work systems (not only in factories, but also in virtually every enterprise offering employment) have been nearly as interchangeable as the parts in an assembly. For a simple job that only takes a few minutes to do competently, the person doing the work has no job security and nothing to look forward to except the end of the day or the week. This creates a fear-driven culture that rewards compliance; "don't rock the boat and you'll get to keep your job." If we are simply encouraging compliance, we are not creating a workplace that drives continuous improvement from engaged team members.

A small change in the design of work (from simple and repetitious to multifaceted), and a small change in the message we give to employees (from "don't rock the boat" to "we need you to be an expert in these few tasks") can begin to shift the culture. If the job requires an expert rather than a layman, it is more significant for the worker. Remember from our discussion about satisfaction that significance is one factor that makes work meaningful.

On this journey to expertise, we have to make sure that people are in fact improving as they continue to work. If we aren't setting the right standards or measuring the right things, we probably won't find out. Keep in mind that working toward mastery requires a string of successes to keep the ball rolling. They don't have to be big jumps; they can be very small and simple successes. If we never get the hang of a new process, the work just gets frustrating. That's why the training has to be careful and deliberate, and practice has to be supervised. Mastery seldom happens just through practice.

Leadersights: Letting Go

Mastery begins with a challenge ("We need to finish this task in 96 seconds or less") and a standardized process to achieve the challenge providing us with a platform or baseline from which to work. Repetition follows. As we repeat the task following the standardized work, we get better with each success. As we measure our progress against our challenge (the established goal) and hold people accountable to the standardized work, we can see their skills improving. As their skills improve, leaders have to lay down a new challenge to keep things from getting routine or mundane. ("Now let's do this task in 75 seconds.") Eventually, the team will set its own challenges and find the best way to achieve them.

To build mastery, follow this roadmap (clockwise, from top left):

Step 1. Set the goal (challenge)

Step 2. Find the best way (process) to meet the challenge, document it, and teach everyone that process (using standardized work)

Step 3. Require that everyone always do the work that same, best way (repetition)

Step 4. Measure progress frequently, holding people accountable to each other and to the process, rewarding successes, and respectfully correcting errors (accountability)

When everyone on the team is able to meet the challenge, set a new, more demanding, goal and repeat the cycle. When they are ready, let go, and let them set their own challenges. Recognize them with every one they achieve.

Vicarious Learning

Whether it's swimming in the Olympics, inputting orders in a database, or taking a patient's vital signs, there are always differences in the way people perform, even when they are all following the same instructions. Some people become experts in certain skills or tasks more quickly than others. Typically, experts will be able to complete a task more quickly or with less physical or mental exertion. In the past, leaders concluded that the expert should simply be the one to do that particular job because they possessed that certain ability. They might be left to do that job for years and years, never teaching anyone else how to do it. The likely outcome is the expert concludes that his job security depends on him being the only one able to complete that particular task.

For the sake of the business, and for the sake of the employee, all jobs need to be shared in a designed work package. The risk of loss in individual efficiency will be more than mitigated by the positive benefits of higher levels of engagement and learning. Chapter 8 provides more information on creating and managing work packages.

Vicarious learning means that people learn by watching others, then mimicking what they have seen. This works with both children and adults. This is the cornerstone of job instruction in a workplace. For self-efficacy to increase, people need to be able to observe experts as they perform a task. Even when an expert can't tell others what they do differently, a careful observer can see the hidden knack points that distinguish expertise. Capturing and teaching those knack points allows others to mimic them and can make everyone an expert more quickly.

Design workplaces so that people can observe each other as they do their assigned work, and encourage people to discuss what they see. This way, each individual can improve skills. Four or five people working together to discover the best way to do their work promotes teamwork, draws people together with a common goal (the challenge laid down by either the leader or the team), and provides arguably the best learning environment for people—one where they can freely share ideas and try new techniques with others in a nonthreatening way. With all of them working together on a series of tasks, learning to become experts in four or five similar jobs, and repeating these four or five similar jobs frequently (at least every day or so), the workplace now provides variety for team members. Variety, like significance, contributes to meaningfulness and satisfaction on the job.

Coaching/Verbal Persuasion

At this point, we have emphasized the need for workers to be experts on the job and provided standardized work as the primary means to build mastery and increase feelings of self-efficacy. We have organized them into teams so that they can learn from each other while they work and interact during the day, as the secondary means.

The third element of self-efficacy is coaching. Coaches do very specific things for skill building:

- Coaches challenge the team by setting an aggressive but achievable goal
- Coaches support the team in accomplishing their goals by providing the resources the team needs to succeed and jumping in to help when necessary
- Coaches correct a team member's improper performance, providing immediate, constructive, and specific feedback
- Coaches encourage people to attempt more difficult goals, and encourage them to try again after a failure

But a coach can only do these things if she's with the team while they are performing. At work, this is an organization structure issue. If the coach is going to challenge, support, correct, and encourage then she can't be one of the working team members.

In lean organizations like Toyota, the best person for this function is the Team Leader (TL). Many people are confused by this title, assuming that the TL has to be in charge of the team. The TL is simply another role that team members must learn and perform. The TL is responsible for several key tasks: supporting the team by responding to problem signals; reporting status at frequent intervals; following up on improvement ideas; replenishing consumable supplies for the team; and observing the team members as they perform, providing appropriate performance feedback as a peer rather than a supervisor, so we minimize fear. If we make the coach the evaluator or judge, then we substitute the positive aspects of encouraging and correcting with more punitive functions associated with supervision. At subsequent levels of the organization, the leader is very likely to be the manager or supervisor, but he or she bears the same responsibility for coaching and developing skills. In Chapter 5, we're going to dissect this role more carefully and present an argument for workplaces to embrace this role as critical to its future success and how to manage this role reasonably, so that they can overcome the concerns surrounding financing these positions as well as build more powerful team relationships that promote collaboration rather than competition and fear.

Control

The final element of self-efficacy is having control over the work environment. People need to feel that they can make changes to those things in their workplace that prevent them from being their best. These feelings of autonomy and self-direction have been tied not only to self-efficacy to but also to satisfaction in work and in life. In our earlier discussion on satisfaction, autonomy and control are translated into responsibility.

By virtue of their positions in workplaces, leaders have both responsibility and the power associated with satisfying that responsibility. Therefore, to provide for this element of self-efficacy, leaders will have to give up some of that power, and share responsibility with their people. While this isn't the first book to implore leaders to empower the workforce, the structure I've just described here to build self-efficacy in individuals perfectly mitigates the risk leaders often bear with empowerment.

With a focus on mastery, instead of empowering an individual, we empower an expert. With teams focused on learning and improving, we empower a team of experts, not just individuals. With a team leader in a supportive role as coach in our team structure, we empower a team of experts with an asset who will challenge, support, correct, and encourage that team (see Figure 4.1). Where is the risk with this type of focused and structured organization?

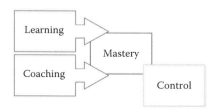

FIGURE 4.1
Self-efficacy model.

MOTIVATION

Leaders hear an awful lot about motivating their workforce. Many think that is their primary job and go about setting key performance indicators, building and using reward structures, conducting personal counseling and mentoring sessions, and completing timely performance appraisals to get people fired up. Sadly, most of these will only motivate compliance and are likely to never get people to the higher levels of motivation that deliver additional discretionary effort to the workplace. What's the key insight for this? Leaders can't deeply motivate people. Leaders can only create an environment where people can become deeply motivated.

Extrinsic and Intrinsic Motivation

Two broad categories capture most motivation research: extrinsic and intrinsic motivation. Both of these require some type of trigger that produces action toward a particular direction, and energy to persist until a goal is achieved. In general terms, the trigger for extrinsic motivation is an externally offered reward or threat while the trigger for intrinsic motivation is an interest or desire within an individual. The truest indicator of motivation is how long a person persists on a task, overcoming any obstacles and barriers as they go. To that end, some researchers have found that the most persistent people are those who are intrinsically motivated. This is where self-efficacy and motivation link together. If we design a workplace to meet the goal of building individual self-efficacy, we will be creating a workplace that can trigger intrinsic motivation in the workforce.

Because we're trying to motivate people to behave differently within a new system, we need to understand the way people are likely to react when we propose some new change and to provide some help so that they will come along, and eventually drive future change. In 1999, Thad Green and Raymond Butkus published a synthesis of several motivation theories they referred to as "The Belief System"* that resonated with me.

When faced with something new, most people complete a quick and private self-assessment to answer the question: "Can I do that?" For example, say I've been an accounts payable clerk and the company wants to move me into sales support, where I have to input orders within a few minutes

---

* Green, Thad B. and Butkus, Raymond T. (1999). *Motivation, Beliefs, and Organizational Transformation*, Quorum Books, Westport, Connecticut. ISBN 1–56720–282–9.

of receiving them. Beyond just wondering why they want me to do that, I ask myself "Can I do that?" We need a positive answer to this confidence question to start the motivation ball rolling. This confidence is what we're after when we design the workplace to build self-efficacy. If we don't get a "Yes, I can!" answer to this question, we won't get any motivation for the change, and the culture will stagnate at a compliance level.

Once we're satisfied that we can do something (or that we can learn to do something that may be novel) the next question is "Will it matter to anyone else?" (Another perspective for this is "What's in it for me?") If the answer to this question is positive as well, people will be willing to attempt the new tasks. In most organizations, the way leaders show the workforce that something matters is by offering some type of reward for the performance. This is both an extrinsic motivation issue and a trust issue. If the individual doesn't believe the reward is worth the effort, or if the individual doesn't believe the organization will provide the reward even if the task is done, motivation evaporates.

With our confidence set (yes, I can!), an extrinsic motivator available, and a moderate degree of value (yes, it matters!), the next question is "Will this be a satisfying experience for me?" If the new task offers something meaningful for us, we can probably answer "yes" to this question. If the answer is "no" to this, we are still likely to get compliance to the task, but we won't get our employees to higher levels of involvement, enthusiasm, or engagement. This is an *intrinsic* motivation issue.

If leaders can get "yes" answers from their team members on all three questions, then the team is highly likely to achieve any realistic goal. There are many tasks that must be done that aren't likely to be very meaning-ful to people. Our task as leaders in these cases is to structure the entire work experience to deliver the most satisfaction possible, and still serve our customers' needs. Don't just let the work happen. Take positive action to create more meaningful work for people.

For our clerk moving to sales support, the reward could be a small pay raise, but in most places I've seen, it is much more likely to be the threat of losing a job that has been eliminated. ("We have eliminated the accounts payable position. We have a position we can place you in with sales support, but if you don't want that job I'm afraid there's nothing else.") Perhaps, a more positive way to frame this is to present the new position as a chal-lenge for our clerk to give the department more flexibility in staffing, and to provide more variety on the job for the clerk. We'll need to explain to everyone why we need more flexibility in staffing, and that explanation needs to tie back into the goals we set for the workplace. Perhaps, this is a step to allow more telecommuting, or more flexible scheduling for people so that they can take better care of their family's needs. Remember, we want to design satisfaction into everyone's work. Variety contributes to that, but work still needs to be meaningful for our people.

Elements of Intrinsic Motivation

How can leaders cultivate intrinsic motivation in their people? Researchers point most frequently to four factors that consistently contribute to acquiring and maintaining intrinsic motivation for activities:

- Competence—feeling that we are capable of doing something
- Affiliation—feeling that we are bonding with others in a shared experience
- Excitement—feeling that an activity may be fun, interesting, or challenging
- Self-determination—feeling that we are in control of our environment

We can easily map these back to self-efficacy, with a couple of minor adjustments.

- Competence = Mastery (we build mastery first with standardized work)
- Affiliation = Vicarious learning (achieved through forming work teams)
- Excitement = Coaching (focusing on the coach's role to challenge the team)
- Self-determination = Control (where leaders fully empower the team of experts)

At work, we can usually spot an intrinsically motivated individual. She is likely to be focused on the work, but seems to be enjoying herself. She may have a smile, unless she's trying to solve a tough problem. Then, we'll see a look of determination on her face. If we stop to talk to her, she will tell us what she is trying to do, and will share with us the ideas she has had, both good and bad. There is energy here. That energy fuels engagement.

Imagine your entire workforce coming to work every day, excited about the day's challenge; excited about meeting with their teammates;

focused on overcoming obstacles and achieving their goals; and determined to make the workplace better. That sounds like a great place to work.

Of course, if everyone is coming to work all fired up and free to make whatever changes they feel like making, whenever they want to, the place will descend into chaos pretty quickly. So, how do leaders maintain their own feelings of control even after empowering their teams of experts? By processing changes through their key learning systems: standardized work and the C4 suggestion system. We will talk about these in depth in Chapters 8 and 9.

THE CONTINUOUS IMPROVEMENT ENGINE

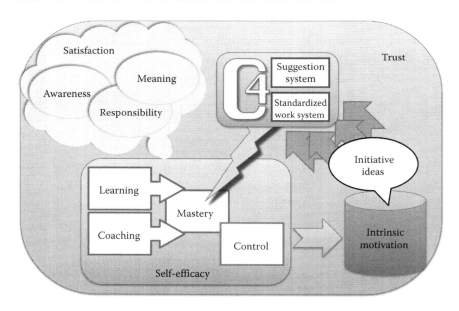

The behavior required to change a culture from one of compliance to one of continuous improvement begins with leaders building trust every day, in everything they do. On that foundation of trust rests the structure that drives behavior in the workforce. That structure is the work itself. Leaders have to accept the role of work designers. Leaders need to engage cross-functional experts in the design of work to ensure we get both maximum efficiency and satisfaction. Those cross-functional experts need to be the operators, clerks, couriers, nurses, etc.—the people who add value in the workplace. So, the leader's real job is to create those experts from the existing pool of people.

Leadersights: Loving

Design work for teams of three to seven people (depending on the work) and arrange the critical work steps so that these people can interact with each other while they are working. Physically change the layout of the workplace if necessary. Assign a team leader to serve as the coach and helper for the team. Remember, the team leader is part of the team, but not tied to specific work output. Document the work with carefully developed standardized work. Teach the standardized work to everyone on the team and enforce the standard every time the work is done. Together these steps initially build competence, and then develop broad expertise or mastery.

As skills improve, people are going to have ideas about improving how they work. To build true self-efficacy, they have to be in control of this, but they also have to have a channel through which they can process their ideas, rather than simple trial and error. That channel is the leader's control mechanism.

With mastery, learning, coaching, and control in place, the outcome should be an intrinsically motivated workforce that responds to the challenges of work with a degree of excitement. They know they have the skill to overcome the challenges, and they have a team to back them up should they run into issues. They also have a team leader to provide additional support and encouragement while they exercise their freedom and control in completing the work.

Intrinsic motivation shows up in the form of ideas and the initiative to try those ideas. Channel the ideas and initiative through a standardized system that requires people to deliberately analyze the work and its problems, create multiple solutions from those ideas, and evaluate the solutions to select the best one to implement. Remember that analyze, create, and evaluate are the highest levels of learning for people! Every time someone has an idea, they work through this process with the team leader or a peer coach. No one has to do it by himself. Repeating this thought process with every idea (good or bad) builds expertise or mastery in thinking and problem solving.

The continuous improvement engine block is the team, the team leader, and standardized work for the team's work processes. Ideas and initiative from team members provide the fuel to power the engine. The C4 process serves as the turbocharger to boost the engine's performance. The C4 process has been deliberately designed for leaders to teach problem solving to their workplaces more effectively, and to drive higher levels of learning throughout the workplace. It is described in detail in Chapter 9. As mastery increases and the team builds closer relationships, leaders give more control to the team and the self-efficacy of team members increases, leading to higher levels of intrinsic motivation, more ideas, more thorough learning and analysis, more expertise, and the cycle continues in an upward spiral of performance and continuous improvement. All the leader has to do is provide an occasional tune-up with a new challenge or a new team member.

The exhaust (by-product) from the engine is satisfaction. Remember that the key factors for satisfaction are meaningfulness, awareness, and responsibility. Building mastery sends a message of significance to the worker ("This work requires an expert; not just anyone will do."), which contributes to meaningfulness. The relationships among team members will build a strong sense of identity, which also contributes to meaningfulness. Sharing the work by having team members rotate through their various work areas and responsibilities provides variety everyday—the third component of meaningfulness. When we add feedback from a coach and visual management systems, we're contributing to awareness. When we empower the team to correct problems and create solutions to problems, or find ways to make the work better, we're contributing to feelings of responsibility. Work designed with enhancing self-efficacy in mind will be more satisfying for people.

CHAPTER SUMMARY

Self-efficacy is the level of confidence a person feels about his or her ability to do a particular task. Self-efficacy is arguably the most important concept for leaders to understand in order to effectively drive continuous improvement and employee engagement. This cuts to the heart of individual motivation for work and for positive change. People with high self-efficacy are more likely than others to do three key things:

1. Improve their personal work and workstations without prompting
2. Try new things others might suggest (and/or accept more risk)
3. Persist after failure

The critical contributors to higher self-efficacy are mastery, vicarious learning, coaching, and control. There are specific, structural things leaders must do in the workplace to enhance each of these.

Leaders can't truly motivate people. Leaders can only create an environment where people can become motivated.

Motivation comes in two broad forms:

- Extrinsic motivation comes from an externally offered reward or threat
- Intrinsic motivation comes from an interest or desire within an individual

The truest indicator of motivation is how long a person persists on a task, overcoming obstacles and barriers as they go. To that end, some researchers have found that the most persistent people are those who are intrinsically motivated.

The outcomes associated with high self-efficacy are very similar to those associated with intrinsic motivation:

Competence = Mastery (we build mastery first with a challenge and standardized work)
Affiliation = Vicarious learning (achieved through forming work teams)
Excitement = Coaching (focusing on the coach's role to challenge the team through effective goal setting)
Self-determination = Control (where leaders fully empower the team of experts)

Designing work with self-efficacy in mind builds a continuous improvement engine, fueled by ideas and initiative and boosted by the C4 process that develops problem solving and critical thinking skills in the workforce. The exhaust, or residual effect of this engine, is employee satisfaction.

5

Teams

The team is the fundamental unit of an effective, learning workplace. Teams allow for strong employee feelings of identity and belonging. They serve as the best platform for learning new skills. They bring a sense of security to members. Teams allow work to be properly performed and supported, and also allow leaders to be coaches. There is a growing body of knowledge emerging from ongoing research on teams and advanced group dynamics. Teams are complicated! In the following paragraphs, I've tried to pull together several of these thoroughly researched, practical applications so that leaders can benefit from the research without having to dig through all those studies.

A team is different from a group in many ways. I believe that two specific focus points will help you to build better teams and a better workplace:

1. Form teams by deliberate design, with diversity of experiences among the prospective team members in mind
2. The bonding agent for those diverse mindsets is a clear and important goal that gives team members a common purpose

> **Teams need diversity and a common goal**

THE CRITICAL ROLES OF TEAMS

Teams allow leaders to involve and empower people. The team structure allows people to build closer relationships with each other. When leaders ask people to get involved in a particular change, it is easy for an individual to resist because it is easy for a leader to single them out if something goes wrong. If people feel like they can be blamed if anything goes wrong, they are much less likely to try new things. When they are working together with other skilled people toward a common goal, the risk of failure and blame is lower, so they are more likely to accept that risk and try new things. From the leader's perspective, as described in the previous chapter, it is far less risky to empower a team of experts with a support system than to empower a single individual.

Teams satisfy needs. Abraham Maslow was a psychologist who is best known for his hierarchy of needs, which he originally published in "A Dynamic Theory of Human Motivation" in 1943 (see Figure 5.1). His premise is that people are motivated (and therefore act) to satisfy needs, and that certain needs must be met before people pursue others, hence the hierarchy. The first level is physiological needs, such as food and water for survival. Next is safety and security, followed by love and belonging needs, and then esteem needs. A modern workplace satisfies the needs of its team members. A living wage, reasonable working hours, and acceptable break facilities should allow people to satisfy their physiological needs. Safety and security are a little more difficult, being met through creating a safe workplace and the ongoing success of the organization. The team structure, which promotes closer relationships, provides for belonging and love needs in a workplace. Reward, recognition, and personal contact typically satisfy the esteem needs.

Teams allow for maximized learning. Successful adult learning depends heavily on individual experiences shared in a group setting. Within a team, individual team members will experience the work in slightly different

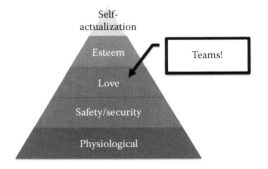

FIGURE 5.1
Maslow's hierarchy of needs.

ways and are likely to discuss these differences among each other. These discussions are likely to lead to better ways to do the work, a more rapid identification, analysis, and resolution of problems, and better working relationships.

Teams expand team member capability beyond daily tasks and standardized work. This is an extension of learning; development and compliance with standardized work is insufficient to cultivate a continuous improvement culture within an organization. Team members work together to solve problems and challenge each other to innovate. They build physical skills for the work they do and cognitive skills for everything else.

Teams provide a support network. Knowing that team members or friends have your back if you make a mistake or don't feel well relieves a significant amount of anxiety in people. Team members can pick up the slack, but also provide enough peer pressure to make sure everyone is aware of who's creating the slack along with who's picking it up. In the Army, soldiers say that in the heat of battle they don't really fight for their country, but rather for their buddies around them. Can we build strong enough relationships in work teams to create that same kind of bond and loyalty? Would people come to work not because the company requires them to be there, but rather so they don't let down their friends or teammates?

> # Build relationships in work teams to create strong bonds and loyalty

Teams encourage taking ownership and responsibility. Workplaces have seen staggering results where individuals and teams behave like they own the place, where people go the extra mile to get jobs finished at higher levels of quality. When there is a clear and important goal, when the team has access to the resources it needs to achieve the goal, and when the leaders stand back and let the team run, the team will begin to take ownership. When the team gets the credit for the results, it will begin to take ownership. With ownership comes responsibility and accountability. The team that feels ownership is more likely to hold its members accountable while still fully supporting them.

Teams promote initiative. With more competence, more support, and more responsibility, people act on their ideas. The team that works together to improve everyone's skills, that provides for everyone's needs, that supports everyone's work, and that cares about the individuals on the team, will pull together and overcome obstacles on their own instead of waiting for someone to tell them what to do.

Keep in mind that for every one of these benefits, a leader can immediately undo any positive gains by stepping in and stopping the team when they are trying something new, or by taking credit for an idea that the team successfully tried. When a leader steps in and reprimands an individual for mistake, or celebrates an individual for the work the team had to do together, that leader undermines the integrity of the team itself. To make teams work, leaders have to allow teams to work. That said, teams won't begin to act like teams without some intervention from leadership. Leaders have to define the team structure, provide opportunities for the team members to get to know each other and each other's capability, and allow the team members to build trust in each other.

TYPES OF TEAMS TO BUILD

A workplace should build three distinct types of teams under the leadersights framework: work teams, learning circles, and kaizen teams. Under all three, the PRIMARY objective is to build team member skills. Keep that always in mind.

Work Teams
Learning Circles
Kaizen Teams

Work Teams

Work teams are permanent teams to which people are assigned to complete their daily work tasks. These daily work tasks should be well documented, with clear standardized work that the team owns and is responsible for improving continuously. There should be several of these daily work tasks so that members of the work team can rotate through the different tasks to enjoy a taste of variety in their workday as well as protect them from repetitive motion injuries. These teams could form in a medical clinic, a steel mill, a sales office, a design firm, a restaurant, or anywhere else work is done.

Work teams should consist of enough people to perform the tasks assigned. There is no magic number for team size, but there should usually be at least three people, and no more than seven for many reasons we'll discuss shortly. All work teams have a team leader to serve as coach and first responder to any problems the team members may experience while they're working. The ultimate goal is for each work team to become a functioning self-directed team, but even then the team must designate one of its rotating roles as that of the team leader. Without that role, we actually put the work (and therefore the customer) at risk, and team and team member development will fail.

Learning Circles

Learning circles are temporary teams pulled together to identify and solve problems in their work area. While workplaces benefit from the solutions, the underlying purpose and most valuable outcome of a learning circle is to offer personal growth opportunities for team members and enhance their problem-solving skills. People in learning circles ideally would be volunteers who have a vested interest and first-hand knowledge about the problem the circle is solving, but because learning circles build skills, leaders may have to be influential or persuasive when seeking volunteers.

Any team member can ask to form a learning circle for a problem they are not able to solve alone or for an idea to improve the work process. Leaders work with the initiator to decide how best to proceed, including who they would like in the circle to help and who might need group problem-solving training, then asking or influencing those people to volunteer. The workplace supports the circle with a dedicated facilitator who helps the circle as they work through the problem-solving process to solve the problem and to achieve other learning objectives. Learning circles meet as needed for specific training activities and to conduct their analysis of the problem, typically 1 hour a week, and typically as paid overtime though some circles meet with no expectation of compensation. Like work teams, the number of people on a learning circle should be driven by the problem they are trying to solve, but a learning circle may also include additional support people from time to time.

This learning circle structure has its roots in the quality control circles movement. These groups are often called QC Circles or Quality Circles. Many organizations tried quality circles in the 1980s and 1990s, but most abandoned them after failing to achieve the results they sought. Many others have teams that are similar to quality circles where people are selected to work on a team with a particular problem to solve. The difference, though, with both quality circles and learning circles, has always been in the underlying purpose.

Quality circles may have originated in Japan in the 1950s when clients of Dr. W. Edwards Deming asked him how they should use their workers when problems arise. Deming hadn't published anything about quality circles and may not have given it much thought, but when pressed for answers, he allegedly told his clients that when they discovered a problem, perhaps they should have some of the workers circle up to discuss what happened, why it happened, and what they could do about it. This brief, offhand comment might have been what led to the development of a full-blown national program by 1962, administered within the national headquarters of the Japanese Union of Scientists and Engineers (JUSE).

In 1966, Joseph Juran, another quality expert who worked in Japan in the 1950s and 1960s (and author of the definitive Quality Handbook) attended a QC Circles Conference and wrote a white paper about his experience entitled "The QC Circle Phenomenon," published by Industrial Quality Control in January 1967. After seeing a team of young women present their work as a quality circle, it struck Juran that this experience was far more than a simple problem-solving drill for the people involved in those teams. How many employees get the frightening opportunity to make a presentation to a large audience, or even a small audience for that matter?

Public speaking is supposed to be one of the top fears for mankind, but here they are; factory employees (Juran describes them as young girls, even providing their names and ages) selected to present their work to a national conference. Juran noted there wasn't anything particularly significant about the problem they solved—reducing the number of loose control knobs on radio assemblies. He then concluded that quality circles were not only about solving work problems, but also about providing employees with an opportunity to grow, learn, and develop. This learning and development focus continues to drive quality circles programs in companies such as Honda and Toyota, both of which report between 250 and 260 active quality circles at any given time. Juran may have made a mistake, though, when in the 1967 article he wrote that companies participating in the conference reported savings of about $3000 from each QC circle and that about 10,000 QC circles had collectively saved about $30 million. At the time, the article failed to make much impact in the United States.

In the 1980s, when Deming's book "Out of the Crisis" was published, with Japanese products gaining significant market share in the US market, and Japanese management techniques all the rage, Juran's article resurfaced, thanks largely to the American Society for Quality Control (ASQC) (which later became the American Society for Quality [ASQ]—where you can still purchase Juran's article today). Of course the American audience, reeling from competitive pressures, found that "$30 million savings" line and immediately dumped people into unsupported QC circles and demanded results and savings, completely missing the part about people development and a focus on the process rather than the result.

Bottom line: Don't form learning circles to solve problems. Form learning circles to improve knowledge, skills, and abilities.

Leadersights: Learning—Forming a Learning Circles System

Set a goal to grow your learning circles system to enroll 25%–30% of your workforce in active, ongoing circles annually. Set a second goal to have enrolled 100% of your workforce in at least one learning circle within 3 years.

Begin small and with no fanfare. Invite five or six of your peers to join you for a discussion before work. Pick a day, time, and place and let them know. Invite them to invite others. When everyone arrives and has settled past the small talk, introduce a "Lean Coffee" technique for promoting conversations and true dialog. Lean Coffee started in Seattle in 2009. You can find all the details you want at http://www.leancoffee.org. I do want to shout out to Jim Benson and Jeremy Lightsmith who are credited with launching Lean Coffee. I've hosted a regular Lean Coffee in Columbus, Ohio, for a while now and it always serves as a great start to the workday.

Lean Coffee begins with what Jim Benson calls a Personal Kanban. This is simply an array of four labeled columns. I usually use the following:

- To Do
- Doing
- Done
- Epiphanies/Lessons learned

Participants write one or two topics for conversation on separate self-adhesive notes and place them in the first column, "To Do." Those topics do not need to be focused in a particular domain in the initial gatherings of this group. People can talk about anything they want to discuss. Later, we'll take the step toward becoming a learning circle, which focuses on a narrower set of issues.

Once everyone has posted the topics of interest to them, give everyone one or two sentences to elaborate on their topic or topics. After this brief introduction, all participants vote to select the order of the topics they intend to discuss. Give participants either two or three votes each, and have them vote by marking the topics they most want to discuss. They may use their votes on two or three different topics or, if they are truly passionate about it, they can place all of their votes on a single topic. The group then rearranges the notes with the most votes at the top and to the right. The top vote getter will be the first topic discussed, so the group will move that note into the next column, "Doing."

One participant needs to step up and volunteer to keep time. Set a countdown timer for 8 minutes and have the participant who wrote that winning note begin the conversation. Others jump in as they desire. Together, the group should ensure that no one dominates the conversation, often asking directly what others may think about the current topic. At the end of the 8-minute session, the group should vote quickly (thumbs up or thumbs down) on whether they want to continue the conversation on that topic or move to the next. If the majority wants to continue, set the clock for 4 more minutes and keep rolling. If the majority votes to stop, move that note into the "Done" column, pull the next most voted for topic into the "Doing" column, reset the clock for 8 minutes, and roll on. You'll keep on discussing topics this way until your planned time expires or people decide they need to get to work (usually around 90 minutes is good). End by asking whether anyone would like to share a key lesson they learned through that conversation, or any "epiphanies" they may have had. Collect and celebrate these.

To become a learning circle, the group needs to focus on a tighter set of topics related to a more specific issue. Within a workplace, pick one key performance indicator (KPI) that you want to improve in one area of your workplace. Next, ask your employees to help you find ways to push the KPI to a higher level by serving on a learning circle. Get four or five employees to form the core team, and then recruit other potential circle participants and facilitators to support the team. Have the team focus their observations on the specific concern identified and have them write one or two observations on separate notes. Then, follow the same procedure as outlined above, facilitating the discussions around your problem-solving process.

Teach the members of learning circles how to evaluate a problem space and let them discuss the "who, what, when, where, and how" to more clearly define the problem. Teach them how to find root causes and conduct experiments to confirm those causes. Teach them how to creatively generate multiple countermeasures, and have them define the criteria by which they will evaluate those options to select the all-around best countermeasure. Then have them implement that solution and assess the results. Teach them how to reflect on their experiences to gather key lessons learned in order to share with other people in the workplace. Finally, have them report their experiences to the workplace in an open forum, pushing them beyond their comfort level and offering a true growth and development opportunity for them. Do this gently, with lots of positive comments, but share these successes.

To provide support to workplace learning circles, The Compression Institute is standing up community learning groups around the country. They are modeling the Lean Coffee structure because they have found that it works well to promote dialogue about often very tough and complex issues. These issues often face communities and are shared among the companies, schools, churches, civic groups, and social networks existing there. As the community learning groups facilitate dialogue from these stakeholders, they intend to capture key lessons learned and share those with other communities through their learning groups to disseminate this learning and keep progressing toward solutions.

Kaizen Teams

Kaizen teams are permanent teams but with temporary members. Many organizations have a continuous improvement group that is theoretically responsible for assisting other departments as they make improvements in their operations. Sadly, this usually creates the impression among some that continuous improvement is the responsibility of the continuous improvement group, and they neglect their own responsibility for driving improvement. With that in mind, the kaizen team must be structured as a training and development group for the people selected to serve on the team, rather than a project execution or problem-solving group itself.

> # Kaizen = Doing something daily to make things better for the people around you

The kaizen team should have one or two permanent gurus, who serve as coordinators and schedulers, as well as coaches for the rotating team members. People who are freed from processes after an improvement project could be assigned to the kaizen team to learn more about improvement, problem solving, and everything else about the workplace. For this reason, the kaizen team always takes the best people available. Team members will learn more about how the organization operates by coordinating and collaborating with departments such as accounting and finance, quality, engineering, operations, and human resources to execute improvement plans and provide additional resources to those department heads and project managers. Projects will come from working groups throughout the workplace and the kaizen team will help them first assess their current work, then plan and execute improvements wherever necessary.

This team can be as large as necessary, but as the number of team members climbs, the organization may need to break them into multiple teams and designate specific team leaders for each. The work that team members do must be meaningful, rather than things like cleaning up and painting. Selected team members will work on the kaizen team for 12–18 months and at the end of this assignment, they return to a working position as a more useful, more aware, and more talented team member or team leader.

NORMAL TEAM DEVELOPMENT

Regardless of function, teams develop through a predictable set of stages (see Figure 5.2) often called forming, storming, norming, performing, and adjourning after Tuckman's theory of team development (Tuckman,

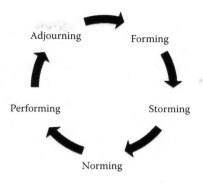

FIGURE 5.2
Team development cycle.

1965). When first assembled, a team needs a charter to define its role and expected outcomes. This provides the common goal for the team members, and should roughly identify the skill sets required for the team members. Balancing the team's work with the demand for its output will specify how many people will be assigned with this duty. Remember that teams still need diversity, even if they are going to be doing repetitive work. Teams are deliberately designed and built rather than simply thrown together.

Forming

In this first stage of development, people are sorting themselves out, learning what each individual can offer to the group, and testing to see who will do what. People are typically polite at first (though not always). In this stage, the leader needs to set aside time for specific team-building activities that will promote this "getting-to-know-you" requirement. The Pig Personality profile discussed in Chapter 1 might serve to catalyze the process. Teams will need more difficult challenges, however, to bond effectively and to progress through these stages of development. Better to have the first challenges offered in a relatively controlled environment, with a skilled facilitator, than to allow teams to fend for themselves; unsupported teams fail.

Storming

As the team members begin to trust each other (or when they get tired of putting up with one or two loud-mouthed bullies dominating everything the team does!), expect some conflict. Some people find it a little odd that early signs of trust include conflict. In many cases, leaders and facilitators try to squash any signs of conflict as early as possible, but that usually squashes team development. Teams that can't make it through this stage will never be high-performing teams. Conflict does have to be managed, though, as there is a huge difference between debating the merits of one's opinion and making contemptuous comments about a team member's mother. Storming is also likely to cause some team members to simply withdraw, keeping quietly to themselves and letting the rest of the team storm on. Leaders and facilitators may have to be very direct in handling team conflicts, and will have to referee when debate turns to argument. Personal attacks are never helpful and require immediate intervention to get the team back on task. Skilled facilitators are worth their weight in gold during this stage of development, and every organization should invest in facilitator training to cultivate this resource.

Norming

The fire of the storming stage forges a set of behavioral norms or group values for the team. As the team employs facilitation tools to work through conflicts, the nature of the group changes. Team members recognize the value of others' contributions. They have a strong sense of individual strengths and weaknesses, and may be beginning to hold some professional affection for each other. With the ground rules worked out, the team can direct each other's strengths for maximum benefit and begin making significant progress.

Performing

The natural progression of team development reaches its peak when the team experiences a series of small successes under their established ground rules and begins performing at a high level. The team will be cohesive and protective of each other, and will be able to attack increasingly more difficult challenges. The team will be largely self-directing because everyone knows, and is comfortable in, their particular role. From a team-design perspective, leaders will need to plan for these developmental milestones and even offer challenges intended to push a team through each successive stage.

Adjourning

A dozen years after Tuckman published his study, a graduate assistant (Jensen) noted that teams do not always stay together (Tuckman and Jensen, 1977). At any stage of development, teams can dramatically regress when a new team member joins or a team member departs. This is inevitable, so organizations should attempt to capture the learning experienced by the team before this disintegration, and plan to reenergize the facilitation of the affected team to get them back on the development path as quickly as possible.

Upon a team member's anticipated departure (retirement, promotion, etc.), make a point to give the team some time to meet and reflect on the impact the team member had on the others, what key lessons they taught and learned, and discuss how roles will change within the team and how to assimilate a new team member should one be assigned. This is a directed reflection and needs someone to facilitate. Recognize the departing person's contributions and celebrate the team's successes. Send off the departing team member or welcome the new one with respect and admiration.

In the case of less pleasant departures (dismissal, termination, injury, etc.), it is still important to draw the team together and work through their thoughts and feelings about the departing member, again drawing out the value that team member provided, and again reflecting on roles and welcoming a new team member. This too is a directed reflection that the workplace should support. And don't forget, you can still celebrate (sometimes the departure is the best reason to celebrate!).

The evolution of a team through these stages doesn't necessarily require a lot of time. I've seen teams in focused problem-solving activities go through all five stages in 4 days. If you have led or participated kaizen events, action workouts, or other intense, week-long activities, haven't you noticed that on Monday and early Tuesday, everyone is saying the right kinds of team-oriented things, being mostly friendly and polite, then come in fighting late Tuesday afternoon or Wednesday after some frustrating attempt to gather data or quantify a problem? Conflict ensues through Wednesday and most of Thursday, when as if by magic, people begin connecting the dots and making real progress, often doing a week's worth of work in a single evening. At the team presentation on Friday, many team members are uncharacteristically emotional and openly complimentary of their team members.

TEAM SIZE

One factor that will clearly have an effect on the speed of team development is the size of the team. Smaller teams have the potential to bond much more quickly than a large team, simply because it takes much less time for everyone to learn everyone else's capabilities. Team size should not be an arbitrary decision. The size of any team should depend on the amount of, and level of complexity in, the work, as well as the length of time team members have worked together, and the skill of the person selected for the role of team leader.

Work Complexity

Teams need enough people to do the work required, but the work has to be organized so that the team doesn't get too big and lose the ability to provide the benefits of teams described earlier. The complexity of the work is one driver of team size. As work increases in complexity, it becomes harder to learn and more difficult to perform, perhaps requiring more fine motor skill or more environmental factors to isolate and analyze. More complex work tends to require a smaller team. The burden for the team to actually become a team through building trusting relationships with each other is heavier because the complex work requires more cognitive energy to master, thus leaving less available brainpower for social requirements. In some cases, an individual may even work best this way. For example, Canon's Meister program requires an individual to demonstrate his or her mastery by assembling an entire copier alone. In another instance, engines for the Porsche 911 series built in Stuttgart, Germany, are assembled and signed by a single master craftsman.

Less complex work allows for a larger team, a counterintuitive notion. For example, an automobile is highly complex. To manage that complexity, automakers break that work into hundreds of simpler pieces and assign teams to complete components, subassemblies, or designed segments of a larger assembly. Henry Ford arguably went too far in this breakdown and when the work became too simple, people lost a sense of connection with the work and their coworkers, leading to boredom, mistakes, frustration, and dissatisfaction (Chapter 1, right?).

Cars make for a pretty easy example. It's more challenging to define work and work complexity in many environments like healthcare or refining, where those subassemblies and segments are more abstract. This doesn't relieve leaders from their burden of designing effective work and workplaces, though; it just takes a deeper understanding and a little creativity.

The secret is to articulate what specific work has to be done and ask everyone to help (get everyone engaged in the decision making). Do not underestimate the difficulty in articulating what work must be done. Even people doing a job for decades often misrepresent what work they really do (mostly unintentionally). Tools like value stream mapping and standardized worksheets help in defining the work as well as getting everyone's level of understanding and clarity in sync.

Leaders break the work down into manageable chunks of complexity that preserve a sense of completeness or wholeness for the people doing the work, while allowing for a smaller number of people to complete the work. A team should be responsible for a whole unit of work wherever possible. This allows team members to see their work from the customer's perspective and feel that connection to the customer. This "wholeness" also helps people feel like they have accomplished something during the workday and can go home feeling satisfied rather than frustrated. For leaders, defining that "wholeness" for a particular workplace can be challenging. We often compound the problem with an abstract measurement of output tied to money or as a yield percentage. People need a hard count of the things they complete. This might be a simple count of the number of patients a clinic sees in a day, the number of fuel trucks loaded, the number of drawings completed or released, or the number of cases packed. You may want to convert to dollars or yields for the leadership team, but the people doing the work need to know they are making progress toward a goal. Keep it as simple as you can.

Team Maturity

The longer a group of people has been working together, the larger the team can be. Be careful with this, though. In the New United Motor Manufacturing, Inc. joint venture between Toyota and General Motors in the mid-1980s, the UAW workforce had been together at the Fremont plant for many years but had a reputation for being difficult. When Toyota began operating the plant, they deliberately created very small teams, usually just four team members with a team leader. This enabled the workers to relearn how to build cars following the Toyota Production System. It also allowed Toyota leaders to pay more attention to workers who had largely been neglected in the past, leading to new levels of trust between labor and management there. After several years, the team size gradually grew to five team members with a team leader, then in some work areas as many as six team members with a team leader.

Small teams with team leaders work well, but create a high density of leaders in the workplace. Most of our financial accounting systems justify headcount (particularly hourly headcount) by output, and we usually couch this in terms of earned hours. An hourly employee who "earns" 8 hours, produced the target output. If that hourly employee is a team leader who doesn't actually work in a workstation, seeing patients, building something, or serving a customer, how do we measure that output? In most cases, having that team leader makes our productivity numbers look worse, and it becomes impossible to financially justify having small teams with leaders; it is just too expensive. But that goes right back to how we are measuring output and who produces or services that output. It also fails to consider all three of the critical outputs we get from a true lean system: higher productivity, higher profitability, and higher professionalism. When we consider things that we are NOT doing or doing poorly now—problem solving, following up with an idea for an improvement, wasting resources because we don't discover leaks or mistakes, or losing time when a team member isn't on her game that day—and the capacity of a team leader who can perform all of those tasks, we'll quickly discover that we're making much more progress faster by implementing improvements and solving problems that save money. Although less directly, the team leader role adds a critical bump in performance for the system, improving productivity, reducing total cost, and creating a better place to work for everyone. The team leaders quickly become the busiest and most productive people in the workplace. This still requires a change in the way workplaces think about leadership.

How does this thick density of leaders help or hinder communication flow and rapid action with so many layers of leadership? If workplaces hold a traditional view that each level's leader is the boss with the need to be informed of everything and holding approval authority for taking action, then things will grind to a halt. But in this framework, each leader's focus is on support rather than power. The job is to get resources to the people who need them as quickly as possible, and let them run. Communication is still vital, but instead of experiencing delays as we send messages out and await their return, the necessary information is posted in the work area and the leader is responsible for going and retrieving it, as well as serving the teams instead of the teams serving the leader. We will discuss this more in the following chapters.

Skill of the TL

We put people on teams to benefit from the learning experience that is possible when a small group of people shares a significant experience. The team leader bears the responsibility for coaching and creating growth and development opportunities for team members. Even the team leader role shared in a self-directed team shoulders this load. The difficulty of this task increases exponentially as the team grows larger. If a team leader has been coaching for many years, has led the team to set progressively higher goals for its performance, and knows how to manage the conflicts that arise in pursuit of those demanding goals, he or she may be able to handle the role for a larger group of people. But even the most experienced team leader will lose the ability to serve when the team is too large.

TEAM LEADERSHIP

The role of the team leader as the person who serves the team instead of as the person served by the team is a fundamental principle of leadership in our framework. The team leader, regardless of the level at which he or she serves, fulfills those critical coaching functions of challenging, encouraging, correcting, and supporting the team members. These jobs, especially correcting, require the ability to influence. Correcting refers to changing someone else's behavior.

In an effective workplace, the team structure begins at the value creation level, with a team for every chunk of work and a team leader for every team, by design. This team–team leader structure and role repeats through the different levels in the workplace, so that those team leaders at the value creation level become the team members for the group supervisor, who serves as their team leader and fulfills the skills-development role for them. The group supervisors become the team members for a department manager, who serves as their team leader and fulfills the skills-development role for them, and so on through the workplace until the chief executive serves as the team leader for the executive leadership team.

The resulting nested structure, coupled with visual management systems and daily stand-up meetings or huddles, allows the workplace to identify a problem, share that problem through the workplace, find the resources to solve it, and deploy those resources all within a very short span of time.

Without the team structure, even very good visual and meeting systems will fall short of the potential within the workplace.

CHAPTER SUMMARY

Teams are the fundamental building blocks for learning organizations. They are, by design, diverse in experience but unified through a common objective.

Teams:

- Allow leaders to involve and empower people
- Satisfy team member needs for love and belonging
- Allow for maximized learning through shared experiences
- Expand team member capabilities beyond regular work skills
- Provide a supporting network
- Encourage team member ownership and responsibility
- Promote initiative

We should establish a team-focused structure throughout the organization, with work teams, learning circles, and kaizen teams. All focus on building team member skills for both cognitive functions (thinking) and practical work tasks (doing).

Work teams are the fundamental elements to provide the information, service, or products our internal and external customers require.

Learning circles develop cognitive skills through finding, analyzing, and solving problems within a workplace through focused dialogue and rigorous application of a well-defined problem-solving process.

Kaizen teams develop people through exposing them to larger, more complex problems experienced in different parts of the workplace, allowing them to learn more about how the workplace operates as an entire system.

Teams develop through a predictable set of stages often called forming, storming, norming, performing, and adjourning. Understanding this developmental sequence can help leaders facilitate more deliberate relationship building.

The size of a team should be determined by the work it needs to do and will be mitigated by the complexity of the work, the maturity of the team, and the skill of the leader, but should always consider the difficulty in coaching and developing people. Keep teams small. You'll build better quality relationships, and ease the burden on the team leader.

Work teams should be the default structure throughout a workplace. Each team needs a leader who fulfills a role on that team rather than being the boss of the team. The team leaders at the value-creating level, become the team members for the supervisory-level team. Supervisors become the team members of the manager's team. Managers become the team members of the director's team, and the directors become the team members of the executive team. At each level, the role of the team leader is the same: respond to problems, develop people, coach, and support.

6

Integral Leadership

After much thought, and despite the title of this book, I've come to the conclusion that it isn't the leader that creates the workplace. Rather, it is the workplace that creates the leader. As leaders, we can shape the workplace culture through structural changes, but we must understand that the culture shapes us as well. This is a very fluid organizational dynamic. Dynamic situations call for multiple leadership styles and often cripple leaders who are unable to adjust their behavior quickly enough. This chapter will focus on creating a new type of leader, one who embodies the dynamic stability referred to in Chapter 1.

All of the previous chapters have built a foundation for a new workplace culture. This foundation will allow us to build a different leadership style that flows naturally from the structure of the work, continuously reassembling all of the working components as an integral unit. I call this "integral leadership" and it embodies the behaviors of loving, learning, and letting go as the essential elements of true leadership—leadersights, if you will (from this book's introduction) in a complex mix of interacting factors.

THE INTEGRAL LEADERSHIP MODEL

The model for integral leadership is a multilayered metaphor that has at its center the key qualities of servant leadership, including humility, sacrifice, and will. Here at the core, the behavior that forms the very heart of leadership, is loving.

The next zone out from the core brings a focus on the development and growth of the people for whom the leader is responsible. The key behavior for this zone is learning.

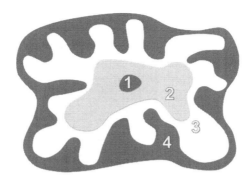

FIGURE 6.1
The integral leadership model.

The next zone out brings innovative and transformative activities. This requires more visionary leadership, along with active coaching. Here, the key behavior is letting go.

The outer zone of the model is focused on attracting others and sensing opportunities. In this space, the leader has to be more charismatic, compelling others to follow. Here, the key behavior is connecting.

I have tried to capture this model graphically in Figure 6.1.

Zone 1: Servant Leadership and Loving

My friend, Mike Hoseus, coauthor of "Toyota Culture," gave me a copy of James Hunter's book *The Servant* (Prima Publishing, 1998) back in 2003. I had been exploring the fringe of servant leadership in my learning about lean systems and Mike had been living it for years; first with Toyota, then with the Center for Quality People and Organizations. *The Servant* was an easy read and set out a pretty clear framework for leadership, one that I thought would fit perfectly within my own vision of what has become integral leadership.

As the name implies, servant leadership is an approach that places responsibility on the leader to serve and satisfy the needs of those they lead. In another book, *The World's Most Powerful Leadership Principle: How to Be a Servant Leader* (WaterBrook, 2004), Hunter defines leadership as "…the set of skills of influencing people to work enthusiastically toward goals identified as being for the common good with character that inspires confidence." Influence, enthusiasm, and confidence in the form of self-efficacy are important outcomes of servant leader behavior.

> **Influencing people to work enthusiastically toward goals identified as being for the common good with character that inspires confidence. Hunter**

The way we influence others is significant. Robert Greenleaf, in *The Servant as Leader* says, "The great leader is first experienced as a servant to others, and that this simple fact is central to his or her greatness." This servant heart is the source of what Greenleaf calls "legitimate power" and is also the core of integral leadership (loving). Hunter emphasizes how servant leadership flows from authority, not power. Authority, he says, begins with a prospective leader's will to love others; to take responsibility for them even when he or she has no structural power or resources other than their own efforts.

Power and Authority

The subtle differences between authority and power can provide fuel for lots of great discussions. These differences are also difficult to define. Dictionary.com uses the word "power" in the first two definition options for authority, and then sprinkles the word "power" throughout the examples given. The main difference between power and authority, to me, is the source from which each flows, but even this is subject to debate.

> **Lead with authority and consensus; not power and coercion.**

An organization bestows power upon a manager by virtue of the position assigned to them. Each leadership position comes with certain responsibilities and the control of certain resources (budget, people, equipment, etc.) necessary to satisfy those responsibilities. Power gives someone the ability to coerce others. Control of resources gives power. Power therefore flows from the top down through a workplace. What some find confusing, however, is that senior leaders delegate "authority" to subordinate leaders. In reality, this type of delegation is just a simple transfer of power through resources. If someone possesses the resources that others require, whether or not he has authority, he can do as he desires. A weapon gives a criminal power to force the store clerk to open the cash register, but the criminal certainly has no authority to do so.

To build and run the continuous improvement engine described earlier, leaders can't simply use their power to make people do their will through threat of force or firing. They have to create an environment of trust and cultivate the proper leader behaviors to build self-efficacy. They need to act with authority instead.

Authority—true authority or "legitimate power"—flows through an organization in all kinds of patterns: top-down, laterally, bottom-up, even across boundaries. Authority allows a leader to lead through influence, with or without power. We see this in many different types of emergent leaders throughout a typical workplace. These are the people to whom others turn for help, encouragement, support, or confidence. The followers in this case make the leader. They provide true authority and legitimate power even when a particular leader may have no positional or organizational power. Authority results in immense legitimate power for a leader.

In *The Servant*, Hunter points to Jesus of Nazareth as an example of true authority. To the people and the government, Jesus had no power (no key resources to control, and no position of responsibility that they could identify), but people said he taught with great authority (Matthew 7:29). Ultimately to believers, Jesus had infinite power but he chose not to wield it, leading instead through authority, influencing people through his teaching instead of coercing or threatening them.

Gaining Authority

A leader's authority can begin with a single tough decision, one requiring significant will. Will is deliberate action driven by intent—a conscious decision to behave in a certain way. The key decision is how to treat people. The way leaders treat others is very much a behavioral issue. Others can only see our behavior, not our intentions, attitudes, or motivations. It is these actions that influence our opinions of people. If we want to create great leaders who create great workplaces that inspire and motivate people for the long term, we have to define and enable proper leader behaviors and actions guided by our values (Chapter 3).

Within lean thinking and in the Toyota Production System, experts say the performance of the system hinges on the two overarching tenets: continuous improvement and respect for people. Treating people with respect shouldn't be a difficult decision but often becomes one because so many people do so many things that irritate, annoy, aggravate, frustrate, or anger so many other people. The more important decision though has to go beyond respect. The true driver of proper behavior is deciding to love.

Most people consider love an emotion, therefore not something suitable for discussing in business. Love is for couples or families, certainly not for employees, right? But love isn't an emotion; love is a decision. That decision can lead to a variety of emotions over the course of a relationship: fear, ecstasy, frustration, anger, contentment. Integral leaders make the decision to love the people around them, even when those people have done nothing in particular to warrant that love.

> ## The key decision is how to treat others... Love

Treating people as if you love them requires you to put their needs above your own. When you love someone, such as a parent loves a child, a host of sacrificial behaviors accompanies that decision. These loving, sacrificial behaviors, as we described in Chapter 4 are

- Challenging them to achieve higher levels
- Supporting their efforts with proper resources and teaching
- Correcting any improper behavior fairly
- Encouraging them to keep improving

It is usually apparent when someone puts your needs above his or her own. It happens every day: when someone else lets you take the cab they hailed; when someone holds a door open for you; when someone allows you to enter the buffet line ahead of them; and when someone pays your tuition and housing bill from college. In workplaces, examples may be just as subtle, but people still notice. When people see that you have their best interests in mind, and that you as a leader have placed their needs above your own, they usually respond in kind or better, providing in essence all the authority the leader needs to be more effective. This, of course, assumes a foundation of trust, which is probably not a very good assumption for most workplaces today. This short list of behaviors should serve as a means to begin building that trust, but the outcomes of this behavior are true authority, legitimate power, and loving influence.

I wish I could consider myself a servant leader, but reflecting back on my career, I can only conclude that if I had known then what I know now, I could have been much better in developing and taking care of my people. I have, however, experienced servant leadership first hand. In my working career, I've had many leaders. Most were very good and a few were pretty bad. But after studying this for years, I can conclude that I have only worked for one leader whom I would consider a true servant leader. Honestly, when I first started working on his staff, I hated him. I worked long hours. He was not very approachable. It seemed like everything I took to him for review, he made me redo, often multiple times.

About a year into this position, I received my first performance evaluation. I was shocked to learn that he viewed my performance as exceptional, when I was certain he thought I sucked as bad as I thought I did. Not only did he write a glowing performance evaluation for me, but made sure that his boss knew that I was solely responsible for the quality of the work that we had done together. When I saw this in writing, I remembered that the big chief had come down to my office a few times to tell me that the work I'd done was great, but I thought he was just being polite. It turns out that my boss, who had criticized and made me redo all that work, presented that work to HIS boss as mine, as if he had very little to do with it.

I thought I worked long hours before this, but afterwards, it became my mission to make my boss look like a million bucks to everyone else. I worked even longer hours, more weekends, did more careful work, finished earlier, and checked and rechecked everything. My behavior changed. My attitude changed.

I attempted to carry these lessons into my future leadership roles with varying degrees of success. I knew that if I placed the needs of my people above my own, if I challenged them to solve the tough problems we encountered instead of solving them myself, if I provided the resources to support their efforts, if I corrected improper or inconsistent behavior fairly, and if I encouraged them all to always improve everything, we could create a great workplace. I'm certain I fell short of what I could have done for them.

Integral leaders, in their hearts and minds, have the will to make the decision to love and to serve in a sacrificial manner, gaining true authority and legitimate power from their followers. This is zone 1 of the model.

Zone 2: Level 5 Leadership and Learning

In his bestseller *Good to Great: Why Some Companies Make the Leap and Others Don't* (HarperBusiness, 2001), Jim Collins described the leaders of his small set of 11 "great" companies as level 5 leaders. Collins said these leaders have three common characteristics or behaviors: great personal humility, a focus on succession for the future of the organization, and an iron will. We discussed will as a function of authority in zone 1, and it carries over, as does the behavior of challenging people, into this zone. Here, though, we want to explore the personal humility and succession focus, because the critical behavior within the zone is learning. Personal humility will lead us to recognize the learning gaps in ourselves and our workplace. The succession focus will lead us through ways to close those learning gaps in the future. These will ensure people have the necessary skills to drive the workplace to a successful and resilient future.

Integral leaders are curious and questioning, challenging themselves and their people to achieve higher levels of development and performance, and building structures that allow experimentation, sharing of discoveries, problem solving, and both personal and process improvement. The true authority generated in zone 1 will flow from this zone as well, only from a slightly different perspective.

> ## Be curious and questioning. Show respect.

That other perspective shows that people consider someone of great expertise as an authority in that area. People will follow others who demonstrate great knowledge, and who competently handle situations with confidence. Earning that brand of authority as a leader begins with a humble pursuit of expertise. Integral leaders seek to understand more and more about their workplace and the people within it, building relationships that allow them to determine learning needs and build the right structures to satisfy those needs. Integral leaders build expertise in learning and coaching.

An effective workplace creates leaders with the abilities to develop and maximize critical skills in the workforce. Becoming an effective workplace is increasingly difficult as the space in which we work continues to become more global and complex. The pace of work continues to accelerate, putting more pressure on people, and especially on leaders, to deliver better products and services in shorter periods of time, with fewer resources and lower cost than ever before.

Our old work habits conflict with the new necessities of our global community, and leaders are caught in the middle. To thrive today we can't rely merely on what worked in the past. We need work systems that allow us to sense problems and opportunities, analyze them, and make better decisions about how to solve the problems or to pursue the opportunities.

Integral leaders will not only need to integrate various leadership styles and behaviors to develop people, but also be effective managers in the workplace. There's a huge difference between these tasks.

Leadership and Management

Here is my take on this age-old discussion. On one hand, managers manage processes. Work processes and systems need management to continue functioning properly in order to provide the products, services, and support customers and other stakeholders require. Management ensures these systems and processes trend toward greater stability. In systems like quality or product safety, this is very much about built-in control. Built-in control systems are designed to create greater stability.

From another perspective, management is often used as a tool to wield power, immediately recognized by people as the enforcer of rules or provider (denier?) of resources. Some people often perceive actions taken under the umbrella of management as unfair or unjust, so the term "Management" is sort of spat instead of spoken.

We do in fact manage through power and control—control of resources, systems, and processes. But if we try to manage people the same way we manage processes, we encounter a host of different people each with unique defense mechanisms, and trying to retain some sense of control in the workplace. No one wants to feel like they have no control over their lives.

> # Managers manage processes. Leaders lead people.

On the other hand, leaders lead people. Leading allows people to continue functioning at high performance levels and provide the products, services, and support customers and other stakeholders require. Leaders ensure that people enable the work system to trend toward more flexibility, keeping the stable system dynamic. Where management flows from power, leadership (as we've already discussed) flows from authority. Because workplaces are full of people and depend on processes to deliver customer satisfaction, leaders need to possess not only the management skills to create and operate the processes and the structural components of a workplace, but also the leadership skills to challenge, support, correct, and encourage the people operating those processes and structures.

The Zone of Proximal Development

In zone 2, critical processes and structural components revolve around learning. I've already mentioned a few so far in this book, and the following chapters will provide more details, but there is an educational concept I want to introduce that will provide some additional argumentative support to some of these structural components. It's called the zone of proximal development or ZPD.

The ZPD is a concept put forth by Ivan Zygofsky that identifies how much better at a task or specific skill a person can become with the help of others. There is a zone of performance that lies between low enough to allow cognitive disengagement and high enough to be considered impossible. The ZPD is on the high end of this scale, running from the point at which a person can perform acceptably to the point at which a person can excel when working with another person of slightly higher skill in the task under investigation. Zygofsky describes this in terms of academic performance of primary school children. Children who are paired with students who have demonstrated a slightly higher level of understanding of the subject reach higher levels of performance in shorter periods of time than those who work on their own. For adults at work, we often apply this to on-boarding new people. But that typically lasts only until the new hire achieves a minimum satisfactory level of expertise. What if we always worked like this? Team structures allow for this kind of paired learning and development.

Scaffolding builds a support structure for the ZPD. Students perform better when they have access to supporting resources in a learning environment created around their needs; like scaffolding around a building. This is a work structure that promotes higher levels of learning and skill development. It looks just like a small team that uses a visual management system to focus on key goals for the workplace. The team is the scaffolding. The goals provide the challenges. Standardized work is the support vehicle and identifies when we deviate from expected performance. The leader then provides corrections and encouragement to team members. Importantly, they also issue new challenges as teams accomplish more together, but only through ongoing and vigorous learning. And this sets the stage for zone 3 in the integral leadership model.

Zone 3: Short-Interval Leadership and Letting Go

I stumbled upon a little book called *Office Kaizen: Transforming Office Operations into a Strategic Competitive Advantage* by William Lareau (ASQ Quality Press, 2002) when I was helping clients understand lean concepts in administrative environments. In it, Lareau defines short-interval leadership as "periodic, regular contact by the supervisor or lead with each employee within an intact work group." The structure of the workplace will dictate the realistic interval and duration of the contact, as will the level of leadership. Lareau was oriented toward the supervisor, but this concept applies at all levels of leadership.

> **Teaching is best when it is personal; and so is leadership.**

The most effective learning and leadership come through teaching. Teaching need not be done in a classroom full of people in student mode. Teaching is best when it's personal, and so is leadership. If we're going to create a vigorous learning workplace, the logical extension of zone 2 is to make effective teachers out of our leaders, then send them out to teach and learn in an aggressive, opportunity seeking workplace that rewards both experimentation and failure, because both enhance learning. Leaders simply cannot be everywhere, so the only way to do this is by letting go and leading through direct contact in short intervals of time. This is the focus of zone 3.

Letting go allows people to find ways to meet the challenges set out by the leader, ensuring the workplace remains flexible and effective. Frequent contact is for correction and encouragement (which are forms of learning as well), ensuring work processes remain stable while speeding up learning cycles. Stability allows us to push the edges of flexibility by providing a safe spot to land when something fails.

Stability comes from rigid structures and well-managed processes with control systems built-in. These boundaries guide independent experimentation when the leader isn't present. From these, we build a vigorous learning system that engages people and makes the entire workplace extremely flexible and effective. This structure demands the right behaviors from everyone in the system and makes it immediately apparent if there's a deviation from the standard of behavior. But the pursuit of learning and opportunity requires complete flexibility as indicated in Figure 6.1, where zone 3 has an amorphous boundary, changing as opportunities arise or experiments play out.

This stable yet flexible structure is not something that a leader can create then walk away from. Just like with everyone else, the work structure drives the behavior of leaders, regardless of what or how he or she may think. We also know that how we think influences how we behave and that no behavior or action occurs without a pre-occurring thought, however fleeting. We have to be able to describe the key leadership behaviors we're trying to develop, and then try to figure out what work structure will ensure leaders behave according to our stated values.

Our work structures should also challenge leaders to improve their leadership and working skills, support those leaders in their daily performance, correct them when they display the wrong behaviors, and encourage them to try new things and teach those new things to others. There are structural elements here that provide protection for people, allowing them the freedom to fail. Coaching involves correcting behaviors that are inconsistent with these elements, and providing support as people extend themselves and attempt new things.

Learning Structures

The primary learning structure is the small team. Each small team has a leader role. Early on, we'll need a trained coach to fill this role, but his job is to teach everyone how to fill the leader role so it becomes a rotational position like any other position on the team. If every leader, at every level of an organization, has this same basic small team structure to work from, there should be no problem making the rounds to have contact with everyone daily. Team members learn from each other during the day as the work progresses and the scope of work for which the team is responsible provides an excellent boundary to guide their experiments.

> # The primary learning structure is a small team.

Standardized work for each role is the next structural component required for zone 3. Some details for creating standardized work are included in Chapter 8. Standards set the expectations of behavior, outlining goals for everyone. The standardized work system itself demands that people continuously test for better ways to complete tasks and achieve goals, making it extremely flexible even though it sounds like it is locking down one way to do the work.

Regular contact is the next structural component. That contact has to deliver value to both the leader and the team member. It has to be meaningful contact, not just a cursory check off a checklist. This contact needs to allow the leader to ask questions that inquire about the progress people are making toward goals, or what barriers the leader may need to work to reduce. This also requires the leader to show true respect for people in the way they ask their questions, and the way they learn from, and teach, others. The needs of the team member always come first.

The frequency of contact will depend on the work cycles. Shorter cycle times lead to more frequent contact, perhaps every hour through the workday. Longer cycle times lead to less frequent contact, but never less than once per day (even for remote sites). This contact can be in person, via telephone, or via video link. As technology and social media platforms change, creative leaders may find ways to use Twitter, Snapchat, Periscope, Groupme, or some other platform to make meaningful contact. These will be spelled out in yet another structural component—the leader's standardized work (Chapter 8).

The next structural component is a visual management system that displays the goals of the team, as well as the progress toward those goals to match the interval of contact. Hourly contact means there will be some measurement on the team's daily information management board that is to be updated hourly. There is a much more detailed discussion of visual management systems in Chapter 7.

The goal for all of this structure is to engage people in the workplace. People need leaders whom they can trust to do all they can to achieve the goals set out, provided those goals are important and good for everyone (remember Hunter's definition of leadership described earlier!). A culture of engagement builds from involvement and enthusiasm. The big jump from enthusiasm to engagement comes from self-determination. That is, when people believe that they are allowed or expected to change things, and they are actually rewarded for that activity (even if it fails from time to time), they will act. And leaders must permit them to act. The short-interval contact is not to keep people in line, but to see what they have discovered and share that learning experience across the workplace. This is true empowerment. These structural components will allow leaders to retain a sense of overall control even when they have empowered everyone to work and create better ways to work. That in turns gives people a sense of overall control of their work life. That feeling of control is empowering and satisfying. Our system for developing leaders, leader standardized work (LSW), has to define this type of empowerment and hold leaders to those supporting behaviors. Whenever we find a leader whose people are not making progress, we have to correct that leader's behavior, and again, this applies to leaders at every level of the workplace.

Zone 4: Charismatic Leadership and Connecting

Zone 4 offers something substantially different. While servant leadership, level 5 leadership, and short-interval leadership all build from a humble base and require leaders to sacrifice for their people, zone 4 behaviors require nearly the opposite. I have two sources from Dr. Jeffrey Pfeffer that have pushed my thinking to add this level to the integral leadership model: *Power: Why Some People Have It and Others Don't* (HarperCollins, 2010) and *Leadership BS: Fixing Workplaces and Careers One Truth at a Time* (HarperCollins, 2015). Both tell great stories about the truth of leader behaviors around using power to ascend to positions above competitors and why, despite calls for humility and authenticity, the reality is that leaders are neither.

I look at it this way; for a workplace to have long-term effectiveness, we have to frequently infuse new thinking into older paradigms. People will always have reasons to seek outside employment, retire, or just outright quit. We will often need to grow so that we can serve new or larger markets. To attract new talent, and often to develop and retain the talent we have, leaders will therefore have to sometimes set aside that quiet humility and let everyone know how great they are. Let's face it; people are quickly drawn to those who are confident, outgoing, and even brash. How else would we elect presidents and prime ministers? We don't want someone who shuns the spotlight and places all credit at the feet of others. We want people who can convince us that they can do what no one else can do.

Leaders, like everyone else in the workforce, need to stand out from competitors and be noticed so they can climb to those positions where they can then back off from the ego trip and truly put their workplace first. Without that outgoing confidence and charisma, not only can we not attract new talent, we also cannot attract new customers or investors. In zone 4, we turn it loose, but never so much that our hearts are not in the right place...back in zone 1. In other words, an integral leader knows that he has to stand out and look like the superhero, but doesn't sacrifice his people to sell that message to everyone else.

In zone 1, our emphasis was on leaders loving their people. In zone 4, people need to love their leaders. From a leader development perspective, it's important that we teach leaders the importance of creating a reputation of success. Our structural components from zone 3 will also provide the evidence of that success, showing clearly how we have set and attained challenging goals, perhaps related to market cap, profitability, or creating the best place to work. But the foundation of that initial attraction is the hard work of building a connected network of people and resources that give us a support system to turn to in case things get a little rough. So while the attention of the observing world points to bravado, the goal is to turn that attention into a meaningful connection that can offer opportunities for the workplace to pursue, whether it's a new source of learning or some way to protect our people in the face of challenging times.

Living in the integral model means that the leader learns to adapt to the changing environment, but always knows that success lies in loving, learning, letting go, and maintaining connecting relationships internally and externally, all through the visible and demonstrated behavior people can see.

INTEGRAL LEADERSHIP IS NOT ENOUGH

We need to be able to attract, develop, and retain the best people possible. But for real long-term viability, the vehicle for attracting, developing, and retaining people needs to be the work, not the leader, the work environment, or the benefits and compensation. Leaders come and go. The work environment ebbs and flows largely with the leaders. Benefits and compensation are only short-term extrinsic motivators—essential hygiene factors, as Frederick Herzberg described them in his classic 1968 *Harvard Business Review* article "One more time: How do you motivate employees?" (issue 46, pp. 53–62). A generous benefits and compensation package may attract talented people, but it still fails to develop and retain them when the work sucks.

Please don't misunderstand the message; I think it is critical that we as leaders create exciting, friendly, social, and productive workplaces. I think it is critical that we pay people enough to improve their quality of life, not just make a living. I think it is critical that we offer a fantastic and well-suited package of benefits for our people. All of these contribute to getting people to want to keep coming to work and to do great things, but the only real value is the work.

The work itself, if designed toward the proper purpose, will serve as the powerful *intrinsic* motivator that drives employee engagement and improves performance over time. We have to design the kind of work that people love doing. Leading in a workplace like this ought to be as exciting and as rewarding for the leader as it is for everyone else working there. In the coming chapters, we'll describe ways to create great work and turn workplaces into talent farms that nurture and grow people into integral leaders, whether they end up in leadership positions or just continue to make the workplace better.

At the core of all work should be a truly meaningful purpose. This is true for leadership as well. For a great workplace, a meaningful purpose centers on developing great people. Great people provide great service or build great products. Remember the framework from Chapter 1—we build a great operating system (the just-in-time and jidoka pillars) on a strong foundation of workforce satisfaction. Satisfaction comes from meaningfulness, awareness, and responsibility, with meaningfulness contributing the largest share. We get meaningfulness from feeling that the work we are doing is significant, and where we develop a strong sense of identity with that work, and when we have a variety of different things to do at work. These are critical design characteristics for work.

> **At the core of all work should be a truly meaningful purpose**

Leaders can only design properly when they understand the work that needs to be done and understand the people doing the work. Understanding the work and the people both require time in the workplace, so the largest percentage of a leader's workday should be spent in the workplace, in direct contact with the people they are responsible for developing.

Integral leadership understands self-efficacy as the fuel for personal and process improvement. These leaders take deliberate, designed action to enhance the self-efficacy of their workforce. Earlier, we described how self-efficacy flows from mastery and how building mastery begins with some kind of challenge. Integral leaders tailor their approach, challenging people based on what he or she knows about them individually. Some people respond by being treated as an equal. Some respond by being listened to. Others need to be dared to go after something. Some just want to be asked.

Challenging people effectively depends on our relationships.

KEY WORKING BEHAVIOR FOR LEADERS

Let me summarize what behaviors I've called for.

In zone 1 of the integral leadership model, we call for loving behaviors, which come out by challenging people according to their current skill level, but always in a positive manner that gains trust and higher levels of performance. In addition to challenging, we provide resources that are appropriate for the challenge as the key means of support. Those resources may include a budget, people, space to work in, time to experiment, equipment and materials, and information. We also support the model through our own interactions with people, asking questions and offering supportive advice. We further call for correcting improper performance and qualified this by ensuring that the corrections are made fairly and with the best interests of people at heart. Finally, we call for encouraging, which influences people to go beyond what they think they can do.

In zone 2, we call for learning behaviors. These most often call for curiosity and a desire to understand people and their work. We'll use this understanding as a baseline to again assert the behaviors of challenging, supporting, correcting, and encouraging. But we can't stop there. To change behavior, we need to build new structures to require new action. Experiment and test lots of options and involve your workforce. Ask questions to ensure people are learning.

In zone 3, we call for letting go. Behaviors here focus on allowing people to pursue the challenges, and supporting their efforts by coaching through frequent meaningful contact. Set boundaries for people and give them free reign within those boundaries. Teach people how to build an experiment and how to evaluate results. Again, this turns to challenging, supporting, correcting, and encouraging.

Finally, in zone 4, we went in a new direction and called for behaviors that draw attention to the successes of the organization and of the leaders, with the intention of attracting others to build stronger connected networks. We also need to build the leader's confidence, just as leaders need to build team members' confidence. This returns us to the discussion about self-efficacy and the behaviors we seek as a result: trying new things, improving the work, and persisting through failure. Let's explore these a little further.

Leaders need innovative thinking to improve their piece of the workplace on their own. We develop innovative thinking through practice in activities that require us to think beyond our experience base. We need to develop solutions that push us beyond where we think we can get and may require significant restructuring to realize. This also requires communicating simply and directly with people who will have to implement your changes. Leading a discussion through questioning will help you avoid forcing your idea onto their workplaces. Instead, listen well; asking questions respectfully to fully understand their needs and help them have the idea that will truly change the workplace. Give full credit to them, but in zone 4, ride that success with them. Finally, enforce the expectations and values with courage. Leaders correct bad or improper behavior.

For leaders to try new things, decide what you intend to try, and then do it. See what happens. Take smart risks, though. There is no sense in putting your team and your workplace at risk when you can run a small trial in a more controlled environment. Spend time upfront defining your expected outcomes and make sure you're measuring a control group as well, so that you can confidently say an experiment worked or not. Here, the result is important, not just the learning. Get the result you need, then develop the process that will ensure you always get that result. Despite the need for results, sometimes you can try things just to learn as well.

To persist after failure, take the time to find the root causes of the failure, not just the symptoms. Work through several countermeasures to retry, and try it again quickly. Be tenacious and rigorous in this cycle of planning, doing, checking, and adjusting. Share what you learn, whether successful or not. Listen to others and give their ideas a try as well.

The last of the leader behaviors I want to pull out is coaching. Leaders coach others to higher levels of performance. In Chapter 4, I emphasized the role of coaching, or verbal persuasion, in building individual self-efficacy and intrinsic motivation. This coaching function falls within the responsibilities of all leaders in an organization. We also described the behaviors associated with coaching as challenging, encouraging, correcting, and supporting, and I've echoed those four behaviors repeatedly in the previous paragraphs.

To effectively challenge someone, we have to know their current skill level, because a challenge is a level of performance that just exceeds our current skill level. This applies to any field and any skill we seek to improve. It should always be a positive experience. If I want to get better at tennis, I don't want to play against someone who I can beat every time. Nor do I want to play against someone who beats me every time. But if I play against someone who is just a little better than I am, I'll work harder in pursuit of the victory that I see is possible. The same applies to running. You'll get faster only if you run with someone who is slightly faster than you, someone you think you can catch (well, that's one way to get faster, but this isn't a fitness book, so I won't go down that path).

At work, it's only a little different. At work, the difficulty is in assessing a team's or a leader's current skill level, then setting a goal that, with a little help (scaffolding), they can achieve in a reasonable amount on time. The goal serves as the challenge.

CHAPTER SUMMARY

Loving is the meaningful purpose for every leader. The heart of this leadership model is servant leadership.

Surrounding this central structure is learning. This space seeks understanding, growth, and development. With this base set of skills layered on the heart of a servant, the integral leader can let people go. We give them the freedom to pursue what they feel is best for the workplace. Integral leadership blends loving, learning, and letting go with an outwardly charismatic style that attracts new people to the organization.

Leadership by itself is insufficient to create a great workplace. We have to create great work for people to do. Workplaces need to cultivate the right behavior for leaders. Challenging, supporting, correcting, and encouraging are all actions that work in cohort with loving, learning, and letting go. Connecting people with effective relationship building completes the model, but coaching is the behavior that works day to day. Beyond these behaviors, leaders, like others with high self-efficacy, need to improve their own piece of the organization, not waiting on anyone else to lead the way. They need try new things, take smart risks, and persist after failure to learn as much as they can from that failure and go again.

7

Tools for Integral Leadership from the Lean Toolbox

There are dozens of tools in the lean toolbox. Most are pretty easy to learn how to use. Some are often conceptually misunderstood and therefore often energetically misapplied. The goal for this chapter is to pull out a few of these tools and share my ideas about making them work better and/or longer, making your people better at their jobs, getting them more engaged, and more likely to create the kind of workplace you're going to need in the future.

VISUAL MANAGEMENT SYSTEMS

It's important to have immediate access to really good information to make better decisions minute by minute in the workplace. We typically think about leaders making decisions, but the people doing the work collectively make thousands of decisions every work cycle, every patient, every document, or every transaction. Visual management systems should provide the information they need to make those decisions. That said, very few things make a leader's job easier than an effective visual management system.

Components of a visual system should be oriented toward more effective learning rather than just conveying information to others. Learning is most effective when our people know what leaders expect of them. These become the standards for performance and behavior in the workplace. People also need to know how well they are doing toward meeting those standards. This is the status.

In simple terms, we need to know plan versus actual. The "plan" sets the standard, that is, the workplace goals, and the "actual" provides the status, or the current performance level in near real time. The "near real time" is significant. If customers require that we process 1400 insurance claims a day in our team, it would be good to know that halfway through the day we've finished about 700. If we're behind, and I feel like my share has been pretty light, I can ask my teammates if they need a little help with some of the more complex claims that may be taking more of their time.

This kind of decision making by individual team members reflects their level of engagement. If only the supervisor assigns work, and only does so by circling the team checking to see who is ahead or behind before bringing in more work, then no one will take interest in what anyone else is doing. Instead, we want the supervisor, or team leader, to record the status—in this case the number of completed claims—as frequently as possible (in "near real time" but at least every hour) on an information board everyone can see from their workspace, and tell people we expect them to help each other out as they pull new work in. This also tells them that it's okay to ask for help when they get something that's more complex or problematic. It works with patients in an emergency department or clinic, with plastic parts in a factory, or with pizzas in a restaurant—anywhere.

> **Visual Management Boards should be visible from everyone's workspace**

The more people know about what and how much they are doing, individually and collectively, the more likely they are to help us see problems or suggest ways to improve our processes. It also helps if people know that the work they are doing is making a contribution to the workplace and the community in general. The information we display in our visual system flows from the company's vision and strategic objectives of the workplace, broken down to meaningful measures for each appropriate operational level, be it department by department or value stream by value stream, then further broken down by the primary process at the value-creating point (hands on the patient, direct interface with the customer, building the product, etc.). If I'm at that value-creating point, I should be able to see that, by doing the work I've been assigned on time and with perfect quality, I will have a positive impact on the things that are keys to success for my overall workplace. I need to be able to see that the work I'm doing is significant.

In order to learn, it is crucial that we put the board in a location where it is visible to everyone on the team from their workstation. That enables them to always be aware of the current status. The board also becomes a workplace focus point, provides a place for our team to huddle at the beginning of the day or shift and gives the members of the team some sense of team identity. Recall from Chapter 1 that significance, awareness, and identity are important pieces of satisfaction.

The One-Eyed Man on a Galloping Horse

My favorite standard for visual management (which I stole from my friends at Rolls-Royce) is the "one-eyed man on a galloping horse" standard. That means if Rooster Cogburn (a classic one-eyed man) rode through your workplace at full gallop, he should be able to summarize the status of every activity he rode past once he gets to the end. That's a pretty high standard. It takes a special effort to present the right information to the right people when needed. People need to see and understand the current status at any given time, at a glance, so they can make better decisions.

> **Remember:**
> **Standard v. Status;**
> **Plan v. Actual –**
> **in real time**

Before we explore a few details, I want to stress something about the one-eyed man. I visit a lot of places where the visual boards are clearly used for management show-and-tell rather than as effective learning systems for team members. I visit other places where the visual boards seem to be for visiting customers or industrial tourists ("look how lean we are!"). The one-eyed man doesn't represent the managers or the visitors. The one-eyed man represents the people doing the work. The visual information system has to serve them before anyone else.

Now, how do you make your information available at a glance? How do you make things more visible?

Leadersights: Learning—Making a Visual Information System

a. Limit the information you post. Only display what people really need to know at that level and at that place in the workplace. That may still be a lot of information, but if it is well organized, it'll have the desired effect. That well-organized layout should be standard throughout the workplace, even when the information displayed will be different for each different group of people. Yes, that means all information boards at all levels of the workplace are laid out the same way; they just have different metrics to suit the people and the work. That does NOT mean that teams can't be creative in how the board looks. Teams at all levels should be allowed to decorate to suit their desire, but the quick perception of critical information can't be blocked by the personalization of the board.

b. Metrics, as key performance indicators, drive behavior. If people aren't doing what you want them to do, it's because you are measuring the wrong stuff. A minimum set of metrics to display should include variations (appropriate for the focus level of the workplace) of the following:

- *Safety*. Post something to show that we care about our employees. Include summarized evacuation and active shooter instructions, and how to watch for signs that might indicate future workplace violence. Make these PROACTIVE safety measures instead of simply counting recordable injuries and near misses. Include safety observations made by employees and focus on prevention of any injuries.

- *People*. If we are truly focused on developing people, this category, along with safety, shares the top priority spot. Include status of team member cross training, vacation planning, and participation in improvement activities such as C4 cards (Chapter 9) and learning circles (Chapter 5). Lots of team boards display pictures of team members along with their names. If you mount these on magnets, you can move them to reflect where people are working during the current hour, and show how they are going to rotate after the next break (yes, people should be rotating through a variety of different jobs throughout the day).

- *Quality.* How well are we doing TODAY? Encourage people to report errors and the lost time spent correcting them. Together, find ways to prevent future errors. Compare your performance to yesterday, last month and last year, as well as with national comparison statistics, but avoid having a dozen bar charts to do this; make these meaningful numbers for your people. Do not give a "parts per million" (PPM) number if you usually deal with low numbers (products, patients, services, etc.) per month. The PPM may be meaningful at the strategic level of a workplace, but it's usually meaningless where the people do the work.

- *Delivery.* These focus on customer satisfaction with the products or services we have provided for them. What work do we need to finish TODAY? How are we doing against that daily goal at any given hour of the day? Keep track of your conformance to pace. How many patients or customers have we served today? How many units were produced? You may find that people like seeing the dollar value of this as well as the raw number, so based on average revenue generated per product, customer, or patient, you may choose to post the money you're making. Watch how people respond when things don't go well. That will give you a great indicator of how engaged people are.

- *Cost.* Every process contributes to cost but many go ignored at the process level. In this category, post the consumption rate of supplies and material, including a scrap rate. Make your scrap metric something people can really relate to. Posting scrap as a percentage of material cost doesn't have much impact. You may choose instead to post scrap in pounds. For health care, cost might best be captured as the time a patient spends in any one department (emergency, lab, radiology, etc.). For services, this could be time lost in rework. As with delivery (above), you may choose to also display this as a dollar figure for the day. One critical thing to keep in mind; this category can't be used as a punitive measure. This is best offered to employees to raise awareness. No rewards should be offered for lowest cost performance and no punishment given for higher cost performance. Instead, focus on identifying causes for higher cost, and solve those problems.

- *Environment.* With this category, we're letting all of our employees/associates/team members know that we care about the impact we're having on the planet. Include meaningful measures like power consumption; landfill contribution; floor space; water consumption; recycled material weight; and fuel consumption. All should be measured at the process level where it's displayed and you may consider also displaying at the organizational level so everyone can see their portion of the total.

    Deciding on what metrics are most meaningful and how best to display them will be an ongoing topic of conversation and you should attempt to include everyone in that conversation.

c. Make It BIG. When you post your information, make it big enough to see! In most cases, you won't be able to make all the data big enough to meet this standard, so use a big symbol instead to show the current status. The best visuals I've seen are large green circles for things that are meeting the standard, and large red Xs for things that aren't. I've also seen some yellow triangles for capturing trends (with the tip of the triangle indicating the direction of the trend). I've also visited a few organizations that just use big red and green dots as quick reference symbols, but these make me worry about the one-eyed man being color-blind in his "good" eye. Instead of telling him what's on track and what's not, all he can see is gray. Shapes (circles, Xs, and triangles) are always better than colors, and bigger always trumps smaller.

d. Lighten up. Make sure your information board is in a brightly lit spot. Show the plan versus actual of your most important KPIs in real time using a light emitting diode, or LED display. Build an andon board (a device featuring a lighted overhead display) that allows people to signal when they are having a problem and need additional help. They should be able to activate a switch or pull a cord that turns a light on so the leaders and support staff can see it and respond. I've seen way too many information boards in dark corners, or in back hallways. Too many are placed in spots where there might be room for a huddle but then information is updated and seen only once a day (or less!). Shine some light on the information people need.

e. High contrast. To make information on a board more visible, use something in high contrast with the board background (you know... light stuff on a dark background or dark stuff on a light background). If you color-code things, which I think is a great idea, keep in mind that the code has to be consistent throughout the workplace (offices as well as shop floor, exam rooms as well as supply rooms!). Red should always mean out of standard (so make scrap bins red) and green should always encourage the right behavior (so make recycle bins green).

f. Simplify. To simplify the board, use clear pictures, simple charts, and focused graphs wherever possible, instead of words or letters. This increases the speed of perception, shortens the learning loop, and allows for quicker action to counter bad trends. Try to make something simpler every day. See Figure 7.1 for an example of a team information board.

Another way to simplify the board is to only display what needs to be displayed. Not everything needs to go on the board, so focus attention to what is really important.

Electronic Displays versus the Information Board

I've noticed something I think is a little unusual. Lots of workplace leaders think it would be cool (or better) to display their information on a flat screen TV or on their smartphone instead of on a board updated by hand. They want to show people that they've joined the digital revolution or something, I guess.

I like flat screen TVs as much as anyone, but the process required to update those panels often delays its availability and clouds the understanding of the folks who need it. People sometimes see an expansive, room-sized set of information boards, perhaps in an obeya, or so-called "war room," and imagine that the manpower it must take to update those printed charts and graphs is nonvalue-added work or an outright waste. "Wouldn't it be better if we tied the displays to our IT systems and avoided all that printing and manual updating?" they ask. I've seen a few attempts at this, but I've never seen one that actually worked to change the behavior of the workplace (the culture) like a manual board updated in real time. I'm not going to say it's impossible, but I'd rather spend time on things I know will work. Ultimately, these boards are less about information and more about behavior. They are the structure of culture change within the organization.

Some workplaces have significant investments in enterprise resource planning (ERP) software or electronic medical records (EMR) systems, and they

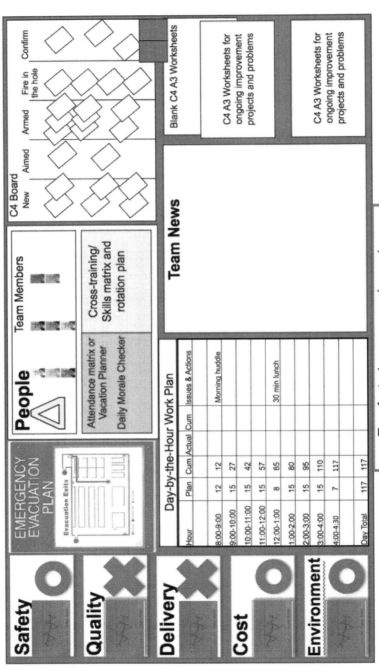

FIGURE 7.1
Sample team-level information board.

tell me that all the data they need are in the computer, and that they can retrieve it when they want it. Too many people, leaders especially, believe this is sufficient for visual management. If someone has to stop working to go and fetch the information they need to determine the status of performance, we compound the problems with performance. I never want people to stop doing productive work to dig out a status report to see where they are against a goal. That should be out in the open, in their faces, and done in real time.

Oddly, the strongest advocates for electronic displays have been in factories and warehouses, while the people who use computers and electronic displays in their daily work (lots of IT professionals) tend to value the handwritten updates to their information boards more.

Bottom line: simpler is better. I remember a story from my Army Acquisition Corps days about NASA's multimillion dollar program to develop a pen that would work in zero gravity. The Russians just took a pencil. Let's not overthink this, ok?

4S (YES, THAT'S FOUR S)

Many people are familiar with 5S as a basic tool in the lean toolbox. It's safe to say that most workplaces begin a lean journey with a 5S activity of some sort. It works pretty well to get people engaged, but the biggest problem by far is sustaining the practices associated with 5S. I think it's time for an update, following the old plan–do–check–act (PDCA) improvement cycle; but first, a little background if you'll indulge me.

The earliest reference I've found on 5S is Taiichi Ohno's first book "Workplace Management." This book was originally published by the Japan Management Association in 1982 under the title "Genba Keiei," translated and published in the United States by Productivity Press in 1988. Granted, I haven't dug through the archives in Japan and the United States, so there is very likely to be an earlier reference, but I really like this one. Ohno is often described as the Architect of the Toyota Production System and is pretty much lean royalty if not lean deity.

"Workplace Management" is a collection of seemingly random stories from Toyota's early days of trying to survive and expand its share of the global automobile market. In Chapter 29, Ohno describes organization, orderliness, cleaning up, cleanliness, and discipline. We get "5S" from the Japanese words for each of these ideas: Seiri, Seiton, Seiso, Seiketsu, and Shitzuke.* Notice that "organization" and "cleaning up" are tasks, but "orderliness," "cleanliness," and "discipline" are all behaviors or habits. With this emphasis on habits, 5S has to be a behavior-oriented system rather than a results-oriented activity. Ohno emphasizes thoughtfully organizing things to support the work instead of simply arraying them to look nice, and keeping things clean instead of just dressing up and painting occasionally or at the end of the day. Both organization and cleaning up have the purpose of making the workplace more useful and better for people rather than making them pretty for visitors.

In the United States, not wanting to spoil a gift of alliteration, we've created our own set of 5S words: sort, set in order, shine or sweep, standardize, and sustain. To me, all of these are chores, or results-oriented activities, and as such, we've lost the focus on habitual behaviors. In conversations I've had around the world with people in their workplaces, 5S always gets interpreted as the cleanup of a workplace. "5S the room" at the end of the day simply means clean things up and get everything reset to the way we found it. This "restart" implies the existence of a standard, which is good, but the ultimate goal is to build meaningful habits. We have 5S audits and have people checking work areas with 5S checklists and assigning scores to post and giving awards, all in the name of the fifth S, sustain. But these places miss the entire purpose of 5S: "arranging things so that they can be brought out promptly" (pp. 117–118) and "to improve the workshop environment so people can feel good as they work" (p. 119).

To me, 5S forms the foundation of a learning system. We organize things, including tools AND the information we present, so that we can learn the current status and compare it against the standard just by looking around. We can maintain the standard because things are where we actually need them to do our jobs. We learn from the system. We learn from the layout. We are more aware of what's going on in our workplace, particularly our role in the success of the workplace. Again, awareness is linked to satisfaction as we discussed earlier in Chapter 1.

I said it's time for a little adjustment to the old 5S, though, and that's why this section is entitled "4S." Okay, so its not exactly an earth-shattering change, but maybe because it's so small, people will be willing to give it a try. The big change is in the sequence, which I've rearranged a tiny bit to reflect the order

---

* I'm not a linguist so I rely on the translators of the book and their accuracy. I did search an online dictionary for these terms and got relatively close hits to these, except for Seiso. A new translation entitled "Taiichi Ohno's Workplace Management," published by McGraw-Hill to commemorate the author's centennial, is different.

in which we actually perform the steps, and the last step, to reflect some hope that we'll build habits around ongoing 4S. Sadly, they are still activities and don't capture the full effect of building habits of orderliness and cleanliness.

My 4S steps are

Sort: We still need to pull things out and get rid of the things we no longer need. This includes information that no longer drives behavior.

Shine: When you clean your garage, you pull everything out, then clean it up before you put things back in. It should be the same at work. We don't set things in order, and then clean them. We clean the floors, walls, tools, and equipment off line, then…

Set: Here we put things exactly where we need them and make it nearly impossible to mess up. This "set" becomes the current standard, so there's no need for another step called standardize. We set, and then reset after every work cycle. I want to stress the need for real structural components for this step. This has to prevent errors or correct bad habits and we can't simply rely on vigilance and diligence.

Simplify: I realize how important it is to build good work habits and sustain those habits and our standards in a work environment. But "standardize" and "sustain" tell me that our workplace is "stagnant." If we are creating a continuous improvement culture, our most fundamental system has to promote the ongoing improvement of EVERYTHING. Making things simpler improves them, whether it's the process for requesting travel reimbursements or the process for building an airplane engine.

KEEP IT CLEAN KAIZEN

Flowing from the foundation of 4S is a need to always keep things clean. In some workplaces, cleanliness is critical for safety and profitability—think hospitals, food processing plants, and restaurants. I first had this idea when I was working with a lamb processing plant in Australia. Any food product that hit the floor had to be thrown away. I suggested that the company could build a campaign around the sole focus of keeping the floor clean.

The power of a single focal point was proven in grand fashion with Paul O'Neill's focus on employee safety at Alcoa, outlined in Charles Duhigg's book *The Power of Habit* (p. 98). While the focus is on one thing, the things that happen to EVERYTHING in order to promote that one thing are pretty interesting. People begin to think about things to PREVENT safety incidents or food products hitting the floor. They might build a screen around a pinch point, or make a splash shield at a cutting station to direct flying bits and pieces to a collecting pan instead of hitting the floor.

We could focus people's thinking on keeping it clean, and then every time they came up with an idea to prevent something from getting dirty, we could call that a KICK, or a Keep It Clean Kaizen (yes, it's hokey... but people respond to hokey!). We could also hold focused improvement activities called KICK events to work together on a particular area that we might be struggling with. Then, you can KICK your heels up at the end and celebrate a little.

The most important point I want to make is this: we need people to think beyond just cleaning up and resetting at the end of the day. We need people to think about keeping things clean and making things BETTER. We need people to think about doing more and wasting less stuff. The KICK campaign could be a good start point for your workplace. Give it a shot and let me know how it turns out.

TAKT TIME

Takt time is a critically important concept that is easy to misunderstand. Issues with what numbers to use to calculate takt time and how to use it in the course of doing work often confuse people. I wanted to include this chunk of the book to address some of the more common things I see students and clients doing wrong.

Takt time is the amount of time we are allowed to take to satisfy a customer. It is always a calculated number rather than a measured number and is best suited for designing work rather than for measuring work. It is simply one of many design parameters that we need to satisfy to create effective workplaces.

> **Takt time is the amount of time we're allowed to take to satisfy a customer.**

The basic formula is Takt Time (TT) = Available Time (AT)/Demand (D), but there are a couple of key qualifiers that will help to make this more useful. I'll break each of them down by element.

Available time is something we can control. Available time only includes time elements, not the number of employees. We get to decide how much time we're going to dedicate to satisfying customer demand. We choose whether to work one shift, two shifts, or six shifts. We choose whether or not to work 24/7, and although some constraints may limit our choices (e.g., it is very expensive to shutdown and startup the hot end of a glass factory or steel mill, so many choose to run 24/7/365), we can limit the scope of our analysis too, and even use takt time to plan for staffing. I have a couple of examples after I cover the demand piece of this equation.

Demand is not really in our control, but we can manage it more than a lot of people realize. It is actually important to manage or we risk throwing our delivery system into chaos. Think about how customers (or patients) show up or order your products or services; some days there is a lot, and others there aren't any. If we release a customer order for fulfillment as soon as it comes in, then on days where the demand is heavy, we might have to call in a lot of extra help, and on days the demand is light, we end up sending people home. Neither of these cases will allow us to create and perform standardized work (see Chapter 8) so our people fail to develop appropriate levels of skill. Instead, they're always in a frantic state of reacting.

Instead, wherever we can (and in some workplaces it is very difficult), we want to aggregate these orders and release them in a regular, controlled interval of time so that we're working at a regular and constant rate instead of surging and ebbing. Because some products or services take longer to finish than others, we have to be careful that we don't release several of the more complex jobs in a row, spacing them out more evenly so that we don't overwhelm our people and have them feel like they are always behind schedule. In cases like lunch hour at a restaurant or Halloween night in the emergency department, we'll need carefully constructed predictive models so that we can staff appropriately.

While we can manage demand, we can't just make stuff up. One of the most problematic cases I have seen in the calculation of the takt time is a client who based his demand not on customer consumption of his product (actual sales), but instead on the number his cost accounting system calculated to absorb his manufacturing costs. One or more of the cost elements in his system really skewed that number, because he was producing probably twice as much as he could actually sell, and when the warehouse filled up, along with all the free space within the factory, he finally started checking things. I never found out what actually happened, but this and a couple of other things completely derailed his lean initiatives.

Restaurant Example

In a restaurant, we may choose to focus on the lunchtime rush, say from 11:30 a.m. to 1:30 p.m. Let's say that we have a fast food place that gets about 220 walk-up customers during a weekday lunch. Let's say, on average, it takes us 6 minutes to take an order, make the food, and serve the food to each of those customers. This 6-minute time is the PROCESS time. Process time is something we can actually observe and measure. Our total available time is 2 hours (11:30 a.m.–1:30 p.m.), or 120 minutes, or 7200 seconds.

Our demand for this period of time is 220, so our takt time is 7200/220 = 32.73 seconds per customer. That means that to get all 220 customers through lunch, we have to, on average, satisfy one customer every 32.73 seconds. How can we do that if the process time is 6 minutes or 360 seconds?

If you divide the process time by the takt time, it'll tell you how many people need to be doing that work to get the CYCLE time at or below the takt time. Cycle time is the average time it will take each of our employees to finish the work required to satisfy our customers. (Cycle time is always a calculated average.) In this case, 360 seconds (process time)/32.73 seconds (takt time) = 10.999 or 11 people working together to get, on average, one customer satisfied every 32.73 seconds. This makes the cycle time equal to the takt time and will give us 100% utilization of our people and resources (which is, realistically, impossible). This scenario doesn't take into consideration the need for employees to occasionally be away from their workstations, which we know is going to happen (bathroom breaks, stock replenishment, cleanup for spills, etc.). We should probably add a little slack capacity to cover those. In this case, we might simply add another person, so we have 12 working, allowing for one employee every work cycle to be off their mark. That will reduce the cycle time to 30 seconds (360 seconds/12 people = 30 seconds), which is less than the takt time (32.73 seconds) and gives us a little slack capacity.

You could also decide to use less available time in the equation. For example, instead of using 7200 seconds of available time, you may choose to use 7000 seconds, perhaps assuming that over the 2-hour period of time, you will lose 200 seconds of actual work time. That changes the takt time from 32.73 to 31.82 seconds. When we divide the process time (360 seconds) by the new takt time (31.82 seconds), we get 11.31, or 12 people (you can't have a fraction of a worker). These figures give us the parameters for the design of each of the workstations in the restaurant. There must be room for that many people to work. Some will be taking orders, some preparing food, some delivering food, and some cleaning up. Each of those functions can be standardized so that regardless of who is doing the work, they all do it the same way—the best way we can design it.

Insurance (Services) Example

Assume in this case we're an insurance company processing policies and claims. Our total headcount is 96 people, including working staff specialists, supervisors, and managers.

Over the last 3 years, we have had to complete an average of 280,000 policies, policy changes, and claims per year. We plan to work 200 days per year (365 days, minus 104 for weekends, minus so many for holidays, minus so many for planned employee focus days or team building, or off-site planning, etc....ending up with 200 days a year that we actually do work on policies and claims). A workday is 8 hours, but every morning we start with a 15-minute huddle to focus on how we did yesterday, discuss any problems our teams are having, and provide a little focus for the day. We also allow two 15-minute breaks per day, one in the morning and one in the afternoon. We allow 30 minutes for lunch, but that is not deducted from the 8 hours (people are at work for 8.5 hours, but only work 8).

What's the takt time?

- Our available time is 8 hours $* 60 = 480$ minutes $- 45$ minutes (breaks and huddle) $= 435$ minutes $* 60 = 26,100$ seconds
- Our leveled demand is 280,000 units/200 days $= 1400$ units required per day
- Takt time $=$ Available time/demand or $26,100/1400 = 18.64$ seconds per unit

Now, assume that a unit of work (whether new policy, claim, adjustment, or modification) takes on average 26 minutes to complete. That means many of these will take much less than 26 minutes, and some will take much more than 26 minutes. How many people do we need processing these units of work and how many units does each person need to complete on average every day?

- Process time per unit is 26 minutes $* 60 = 1560$ seconds
- Dividing 1560 by the takt time 18.64 seconds $= 83.69$ or a total of 84 people are needed to lower the cycle time to a level below the takt time
- Each person needs to complete about 17 units a day to keep up with demand (1400 units/84 people $= 16.667$ units per person per day)

If the processing time creeps up to 30 minutes on average, we end up needing 13 MORE people to satisfy the demand. (30 minutes $* 60 = 1800$ seconds/18.64 $= 96.56$ people required.) If we can improve our process and remove any waste (remember the WORMPIT!) dropping the average process time to 24 minutes (just 2 minutes faster on average), we can satisfy this demand with only 78 people. If the average burdened salary for these team members is $75,000 a year, and we can achieve this lower headcount through natural attrition or by redeploying those six team members to another cost center in the company, we'll save the department $450,000 annually; just from saving 2 minutes from the average process time!

Another issue we have to consider in this is the variety of work tasks within a company. I said some units of work are more complex and therefore more time consuming than others. Sometimes, an experienced team member or supervisor can scan the requirement and identify it as complex or easy fairly quickly. What we have to avoid is the assignment of too many complex cases to one team (or worker) and we especially want to avoid giving someone two or three complex cases back to back. Why? Because our visual board for our team will be showing everyone how many we expect them to finish in the day, and how many they have finished. (See Figure 7.3 a few pages back.) If we assign too many difficult ones back to back, someone will be behind all day and that is often very frustrating. We may choose to segregate the work so that one team does only complex work and other teams do relatively simple work, but that would tend to undermine our intention to develop everyone's skills.

Summary

1. Takt time is the amount of time we are *allowed* to take to satisfy customer demand.

2. Process time is the amount of time *it actually takes* for a worker to satisfy a customer. This is something you can watch and time.
3. Cycle time is the average amount of time it takes *each of our workers* to satisfy each of our customers. Cycle time is always a calculated average.
4. Cycle time must be less than or equal to takt time or we can't satisfy demand. When cycle time equals takt time, we will have 100% utilization, which is usually unsustainable.

THREE-BIN REPLENISHMENT

Lots of places are using two-bin systems to replenish consumable supplies (medical supplies, fasteners, etc.). They work well and have helped lots of people manage their materials better. For my StrikeFighter Simulation, which uses Lego® blocks and simulates a multitiered supply chain that builds and delivers completed airplanes to a customer, I developed a replenishment kit to deliver the required Legos to each of the value-adding workstation. We use three identical kit trays for each workstation, hence "three-bin replenishment." It works great in the simulation but I haven't seen anyone try something quite like this in a workplace. Let me try to describe it, and then if you are doing something like this or if you decide to run an experiment to see if it will work in your workplace, maybe you'll let me know.

Support systems like replenishment have to focus on making the value-adding work better, even at the expense of certain other functions. I might deliberately increase transportation distances to provide a better presentation of work to the assembly work cell or the staff specialist processing the insurance claim, or the dental hygienist cleaning someone's teeth. Despite what you may have learned about lean thinking, it isn't just about eliminating waste; it's really about creating value.

The objectives of the three-bin system are to lower overall levels of inventory, provide better presentation of materials to the people doing the work, and to synchronize various elements of the system to make problems immediately evident so that we can solve them. First, I'll describe how it works in the simulation, and then I'll describe how it might work in a hospital.

In the first round of the simulation, work is split up among functional departments. We move Lego pieces and work-in-process (partially assembled components) into each department in the required sequence, complete the work required by that department, then move the work-in-process to the next until the subassembly is finished and inspected. All inputs for the product are available and accessible to the team and under their control (all required parts are in their warehouse space).

Prior to the second round, we teach participants about creating flow through co-location of resources, reducing batch sizes, balancing work to the takt time, and dedicating appropriate resources where needed. The shorthand version of this is "One Place, One Piece, One Pace, One Source." The "one place" step directs participants to build work cells that include all required resources (equipment, people, parts, information, etc.) then arrange the work cells to achieve flow through their whole facility (or table top in case of the simulation). We decide what to build in each cell so that we can provide exactly what the customer needs exactly when they need it.

In rounds 2 and 3, raw materials come from a variety of suppliers rather than each group already holding the materials they need. The takt time for the system is 1 minute, so the work content (the number of Lego pieces that the cell needs to assemble) is balanced to be just less than 1 minute. That means the replenishment cycle also has to be less than 1 minute. Round 2's performance is always pretty disastrous, as teams are consumed with identifying sources, preparing purchase orders, and trying to work within conventional supply chain and logistics practices despite having applied some lean thinking to their focused work (assembling the aircraft system).

For round 3, to increase the likelihood that the replenishment cycle can function within the takt time, we've built trays with cutouts for every piece the work cell needs. As shown in Figure 7.2, the trays serve as the kit boxes, as well as build boards (assemblers can build the subassembly right on the board). In the simulation, we also refer to them as purpose-built trucks that make the replenishment runs.

Parts for the trays come from four different vendors around the room. All the vendors are color coded (this is very simple to do when there are only four; it is much more challenging when there are hundreds of vendors) so parts supplied by the yellow, red, blue, and green teams will all be marked accordingly. The tray represents the current best way to assemble the pieces, following the standardized work. This allows anyone to step into that work cell and be able to confidently build that component with a minimal amount of training. It is visually driven; besides the tray, we'll display pictures of the build sequence at the work cell to help as well, and

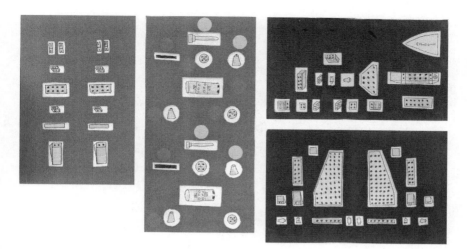

FIGURE 7.2
Kit/build boards.

then regulate the flow with an inbound kanban for each set of materials and an outbound kanban for each finished subassembly.

We begin round 3 with no materials in the system and run until all the kanbans are full, completely loading the work system we've designed. At this point, there are either finished goods or subassemblies in each outbound kanban, a full tray of parts in each inbound kanban, a full tray of parts waiting to be delivered, and an empty tray waiting to be filled. The final activity begins by pulling the finished aircraft from the delivery kanban, which triggers final assembly to pull the main subassemblies from their kanban, which signals the suppliers to deliver the next unit, emptying their delivery kanbans and triggering work cells to begin work. As the work cells pull the trays of parts into the workstations, the truck drivers immediately deliver the waiting trays, pick up the empty ones, and begin their replenishment route. When the work cell completes their assembly work, they place the empty tray in the pickup zone and wait for their customer to pull their subassembly from the outbound kanban so they can build the next. The truck driver fills the tray by visiting each supplier station in turn and placing the required pieces in their designated spaces. Their last stop is their own team's warehouse to retrieve the final parts to fill the kit, and finally delivers the full kit to the inbound kanban for each work cell, picks up the empty trays from the pick-up zone, and begins the replenishment cycle again. If they complete the replenishment cycle within the takt time, they will wait to deliver the full kit until the operator pulls the previous full kit. See Figures 7.3 and 7.4.

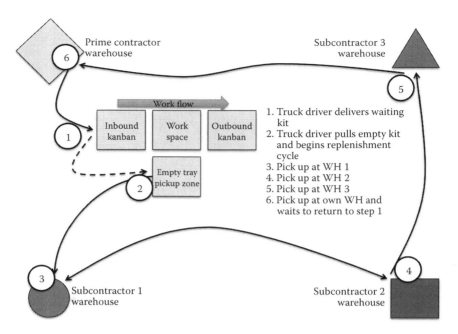

FIGURE 7.3
Replenishment route.

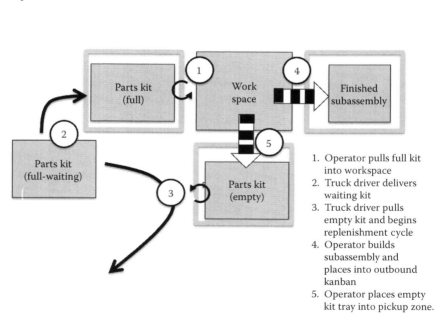

FIGURE 7.4
Three-bin flow.

If, as in most real cases, the replenishment cycle exceeds the takt pace, we need to calculate the number of containers we need in the system to allow for regular replenishment at the takt interval. This is actually a pretty common practice using returnable containers with external suppliers, but see the example for health care below to see whether you may be able to use this to bring work to people in a balanced way. I guess the emphasis I want to add is to study the replenishment of work and materials as diligently as you would study the value-added work. If we apply lean principles of work organization to minimize waste and delays in designing this work targeting the takt time, we should be able to substantially improve performance.

Three-Bin Replenishment in Health Care

Remember that our goal is to make nonrepetitive, long-cycle time work steadier and more balanced so that we can create more effective standardized work, improve employee skills, cross-train better, and create more satisfying work for people. It takes a creative mind to build meaningful and satisfying work out of some jobs, but this might help.

In health care, we're already used to having strict setups for tools and materials necessary for surgical procedures. There will be multiple trays with an exact count of all the different instruments and supplies the surgeon needs to complete the procedure. Staff will carefully keep track of each hemostat, gauze pad, etc. so they can confirm that nothing has been left inside the patient. But for other consumable supplies in different clinical areas where it's less important, our systems aren't so well organized.

The three-bin system begins here by creating modules of supplies based on typical, average consumption with a safety factor included. With a two-bin system, a supply room (or rooms) for the clinic/floor/ward will have shelves full of individual bins stuffed with all the different types of devices and consumable supplies they use (or may use). There will be a full bin behind the bin in use. People remove supplies from the front bin as they need them and when the first bin is empty, they usually put the empty bin on the top shelf of the rack and pull the second, full bin forward. Supply replenishment people will check the room during their morning or afternoon rounds, pick up the empty bins (which are labeled with the appropriate item identifier) and take them back to central stores where they will be filled and returned to the floor on the next day or so, when they make the next replenishment round. Fast-moving supplies can be replenished every day and may even run out and require an expedited replenishment. Slow-moving supplies might sit in the supply room until well past their expiration date.

With the three-bin system, we break the day into several chunks. We can do this by checking to see how long it takes to complete one replenishment cycle through all supply areas or points of use. The strong preference is to replenish points of use rather than a supplemental supply room because we want staff to have what they need at an arm's length instead of having to burn time fetching supplies. We will build a kit of consumable supplies that will last the duration of a replenishment cycle. Let's say it takes the "water spider"* 2 hours (120 minutes) to hit all points of use on two hospital floors. This time includes starting in central stores, traveling with all the kits needed for the floor, dropping each at the required point of use, and returning to central stores for the next load. Our kit will contain enough consumable supplies, devices, or medicine to last for those 2 hours. The water spider will have a kit for each stop arranged in sequence on a cart. If we have sized the kit correctly, when he drops off a full kit, there should be an empty or mostly empty kit that he or she will pick up. So instead of taking bulk supplies and stuffing them into a bin, he takes the whole kit.

While the water spider is making rounds, another is filling kit boxes down in central stores for all the points of use and staging them for eventual pick up by the water spiders. This person pays particular attention to things like expiration dates. With this system, we can add an item that expires tomorrow because our plans show they will be consumed today.

With the three-bin system, there is one bin (kit) at the point of use, one on the cart in transit, and one being filled. We'll be able to consume less space on the floors (no more supply closets or hoarding), freeing that floor space for other purposes. Staff will lose less time being away from their patients to get supplies. Water spiders will have a way to do a variety of tasks and rotate through them throughout the day. We should be able to operate with fewer of them and keep their work more balanced and regular so problems are immediately evident and the work is easier to teach as new people come on board. This system would be perfect for any lab that is already short on space (and that would be every lab I have ever been in!).

---

* Water spider is the term often given to replenishment staff who make multiple stops to pick up and deliver materials in a given space.

CHAPTER SUMMARY

In this chapter, I've shared some ideas to try to get better results from familiar lean tools and to try to push for the evolution of well-known tools so they are easier to teach, easier to learn, and more likely to sustain.

Visual management systems—designed to provide accurate, critical information to the people who need that information in the course of doing their work.

We described several ways to make information more visible (easier to see):

- Limit the information you post. Only post what the target audience needs to see.
- Use the right metrics to drive the right behavior. Monitor and adjust continuously.
- Make the information BIG. Big is easier to see than small.
- Shine some light on your information so it is easier to see.
- Make sure the information is in high contrast to the background of the board (i.e., dark symbols and words on a light board, or light symbols and words on a dark board).
- Try to simplify the presentation of the information every day.

We also discussed electronic displays versus a traditional board. Continue the debate in your lean workplace.

4S versus 5S: It's time to evolve this old system so it becomes a habit-building supportive work system instead of a housekeeping task.

KICK: Okay, it's corny. But corny WORKS!

Takt time: It is critical to understand and use takt time appropriately. Remember, its greatest utility is as a work design parameter.

Three-bin replenishment: I think there is real potential here to design better work for people in supporting roles within any work system. We can reduce the total amount of stuff we have on hand in any given area, saving space and saving staff time.

8

Standardized Work for Processes and Leaders

Standardized work is the single most important system in the continuous improvement world. Like many other concepts in lean systems, standardized work is less of a tool and much more a systemic change. In a continuous improvement environment, we need disciplined people to do their work with minimal variance. Creating and enforcing standardized work helps to ensure this. We need repetitious performance because it builds individual mastery and therefore enhances self-efficacy, which empowers people to act (see Chapter 4). Repetitious performance also reveals problems in the design of the work, regardless of who is actually performing the work in a particular place.

People make arguments against the need for standardized work for nonrepetitive work in administrative, transactional, or healthcare workplaces. But even when a particular job is not especially repetitive, standardized work will help us to ensure that people are able to perform a function when necessary at the right quality level, within a given time standard, and are able to make improvements to their work as they discover new ways to complete the required tasks. It is the combination of those nonrepetitive tasks into work packages featuring different patterns and sequences of work that will allow leaders to design and build full and meaningful workdays for people in these workplaces. These work packages of multiple, nonrepetitive tasks completed in short intervals of time are also important for leaders.

The greatest value in standardized work is ultimately in the freedom of the people doing the work to see and solve problems in their work package, find better ways to do the work, test them, implement them as a new standard, and teach other team members how to do the work the new way. To get to that valuable problem-solving ability it will be necessary to redesign many, if not all, of the pieces within your work system. You can't just document the way you're doing work now and expect that to have any impact. The key will be to design new work packages, document that work, and teach them to the workforce.

My colleagues Parthi Damodaraswamy and Jon Yingling wrote a wonderful book called *Creating and Sustaining Highly Effective Lean Standardized Work Systems*, in which they provide details about restructuring work around work packages. This little book needs a lot more attention from the improvement community and perhaps the public. Much of this chapter will have either been derived from contents of that book, or lifted directly from it. Hopefully, you'll see a need to further understand standardized work after reading this chapter, and then you'll go buy Parthi and Jon's book and start making real progress.

THE PHILOSOPHY BEHIND STANDARDIZED WORK

The leadersights framework outlined in Chapter 1 flows from lean thinking and a deep investigation into the engineering and behavioral theories that underlie the Toyota Production System. Lean and standardized work go hand in hand. You simply can't be lean without standardized work, and you can't do standardized work without becoming lean. This work system forms a strong foundation for building vigorous learning practices that will equip any workplace to thrive in an uncertain future.

> **You simply can't be lean without standardized work, and you can't do standardized work without becoming lean**

Lean is a philosophy in itself. More specifically, it is a people-oriented philosophy that drives success by constantly creating greater value. This definition provides a more positive message for people over other definitions of lean that typically focus on eliminating waste. Yes, we still need to eliminate waste wherever we can find it, but this definition slants the purpose toward people rather than processes, and while these go hand in hand in an integrated system, it's the people who need to hear the positive message. Processes don't seem to mind.

> **Lean is a people-oriented philosophy that drives success by constantly creating greater value**

There are three key outcomes of this type of philosophy:

1. *Higher productivity.* We usually measure productivity in terms of something being faster, better, or easier. We want to get more output of better quality from either the same resources or fewer, or get the same output from significantly fewer resources.
2. *Higher profitability.* We can gain more profit by removing waste and cost from our products and processes and by making our products more attractive either through higher quality levels at less cost or through more reliable and quicker customization and delivery, which makes us more competitive in a global marketplace.
3. *Higher professionalism.* A highly professional workforce means high levels of employee engagement in their work and less turnover or absenteeism because we create a great place to work that attracts and retains better talent. This system should make people want to come to work.

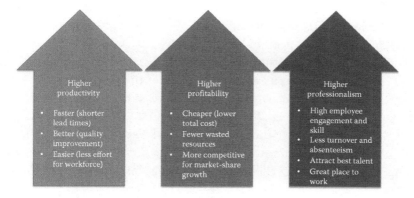

Higher productivity
- Faster (shorter lead times)
- Better (quality improvement)
- Easier (less effort for workforce)

Higher profitability
- Cheaper (lower total cost)
- Fewer wasted resources
- More competitive for market-share growth

Higher professionalism
- High employee engagement and skill
- Less turnover and absenteeism
- Attract best talent
- Great place to work

As a practitioner and coach, my experience has shown that higher productivity and higher profitability are pretty easy to get with regular lean tools, regardless of the messaging behind the effort. Professionalism is always harder because the first two usually threaten the livelihood of employees. In most cases, higher productivity and profitability focus on reducing labor cost (often even when labor is a much smaller portion of the total cost). If after balancing and redesigning work that used to take six people, four people can get the same output, what happens to those two "extra" people? If the focus is exclusively on profitability, we will need to immediately reduce the headcount and eliminate that cost by terminating them. Of course, the survivors will then rightly conclude that headcount reduction is the main goal and will immediately stop helping to drive improvement. Without their help, we can't develop and use effective standardized work, nor will we be able to build the most effective work system.

If we believe that we are creating a new philosophy rather than just running another change initiative; and if we understand that our philosophy forms our way of thinking; and if we recognize that only people can think and therefore create solutions, then to succeed with this we have to focus on people. Gaining higher professionalism means taking the time to develop people. Developing people requires leaders to

- Improve people by building their cognitive and technical skills.
- Create a just and equitable workplace; a place where one can work for an entire career, a place where contributions are solicited and appreciated, and a place where we meet the needs of our people as well as the needs of our customers.
- Create a satisfying workplace with a clear and meaningful purpose, transparency of goals and performance, accountability, and responsibility as we described in Chapter 2.

Creating standardized work meets all of these requirements.

Developing skills in people also drives workplaces through cultural evolution from compliance, through involvement and enthusiasm to engagement. The result, as discussed in Chapter 3, is the conscious decision of every engaged worker to bring his or her discretionary effort to work. That effort—which shows up as those things we DO in the workplace—defines the culture. The culture either makes our workplace great or horrible.

To change that culture, we have to change our thinking—we have to change the way we make those conscious decisions. That must begin with leaders changing the way they think, otherwise it is impossible to change the way anyone else thinks. It is nearly impossible to change how we think without also changing what we do. If we make that conscious decision to lead differently, but have no structural support in the workplace, it is too easy in challenging and stressful times to fall back on what we've done before whether or not it was successful.

New work structures with standardized work, properly executed, require us to change what we as leaders do, and what we have our people do. These will also allow us to get people engaged in making the change with us. Together, these actions, over time, will lead to new mindsets and drive new thinking as people experience success from the new processes.

Developing standardized work makes us change the work we do, changing our actions to achieve consistently better results, which in turn will change how we think about work. The system builds technical and cognitive mastery, forces us to restructure work around work packages that require small teams to work together, allows people to learn from each other, and gives control of the workspace to the people doing the work. These all combine to build self-efficacy, which, as we learned previously, motivates and empowers people to improve their own work, to try new things, and to persist through failures.

FIVE GOALS OF STANDARDIZED WORK

I've included a brief summary for each of the five goals specified in Jon and Parthi's book. Please refer to it for additional details you may need.

Make Tacit Knowledge Explicit

Human beings are remarkably capable of devising creative ways to accomplish tasks. In organizations where no standards exist or are hidden or obsolete, people will find the best way to do the work. It is often very effective, but just as often leads to defects and/or errors, and will always lead to excess variability, as different people doing the same work will typically do that work their own way. Our goal is to focus on the work, not the workers, and to find the very best way to do that work, creating a package of tasks that we will then teach everyone who needs to do the work that best way. Some "experts" hold their ability to do quality work as a protective measure, assuming that if they are the only ones capable of performing a certain task, the company won't be able to fire them or lay them off. This makes capturing the best way to do work both a relationship-building and a trust-building activity as much as a standardized work activity. Observe lots of people doing the work or task you are trying to understand and document. Be open about the purposes of stabilizing the work environment, and do everything you can to assure all of them that the goal is not to remove the experts and replace them with lower-cost workers.

Build in Control

In the redesign of our work into work packages, we need to create flow and regulate that flow to avoid working on anything except what the customers need. We want the structures in the workspace to give us that control of the work, and ideally these will be visual structures like a kanban so everyone can see that we are authorized to do the work we are doing, and we stop when we are finished. Kanban can take many different forms, from electronic signals, to squares marked off with masking tape on a desk to show where completed work should go.

Focus on Methodology

Jon and Parthi make a clear distinction between process technology and methodology technology in their book. The process technology is the specific tool used to perform a specific task, such as a drill bit to drill a hole in a board. We aren't really interested in changing the way the drill bit creates that hole. However, to bring the board and the drill bit together, there are hundreds of different methods for doing that. This is the methodology. Focus on improving the steps leading up to and carrying away from the actual technological process and you can make great progress.

Simplify

You would think simplifying a task would be relatively easy and that most people would understand what you mean when you ask them to simplify the work they do. The truth is that simplifying work is very difficult. For standardized work, here are a couple of things to guide your thinking as you try to simplify the work people do:

- Reduce motion. You'll never eliminate this but give careful thought to how far someone has to reach to be able to do the work, whether it is across a desk, or to the top shelf of a supply cabinet.
- Reduce the need for fine dexterity in holding or working on something. Mind how tightly something needs to be held in doing the work. There are many opportunities for this in health care and food service if we look at how their actual work has to be done.
- Eliminate multiple handling. It is always better to only move something once.
- Reduce the number of decisions a person has to make in completing the work. More decisions typically increase the risk of making an error.
- Remove ambiguity from work execution. This goes hand in hand with the decisions. If after doing my work I have to judge whether it is good enough or not, that mental burden gets exhausting. Find a way to make it simple and clear.

Go beyond Skill

When we think of skilled workers, we usually think of those who are diligent and hardworking, perhaps possessing great dexterity and able to handle delicate work with ease, and those who possess good judgment with respect to the work they do, making better decisions than others. These are wonderful capabilities that we want to enhance in our workforce, but we don't want the successful accomplishment of the work to depend on these. Instead, we want good processes that can turn out good work, regardless of who is actually doing the work. If the process is robust and unambiguous, it won't require a diligent or "disciplined" worker with good judgment to work successfully. By freeing up this mental capacity, we want to enable the people to devote some thinking to discovering better ways to do the work rather than consume their brainpower in just getting the work done. This is an important aspect in turning over control to them and enhancing self-efficacy.

GENERAL GUIDELINES FOR DEVELOPING STANDARDIZED WORK

Here are some guidelines for creating standardized work for processes and for leaders. Sometimes you'll need to get a little creative. Keep in mind that the process of developing the standardized work is more helpful than the finished document set. The deliberate focus required during this process forces us to really understand the work that we need to do.

Let me emphasize this… Standardized work is NOT simply about documenting how you do the work. It is about CHANGING the way you do work and building multi skilled teams that solve their own problems and make their own improvements. That starts with understanding how we do it now, but has to lead to creating more effective and satisfying work packages. The work package is the building block for a successful lean workplace, and the basic working structure for a vigorous learning organization (VLO). Let's get started!

Doing This Will Take a Long Time

Go into this understanding that developing standardized work will take a long time. There are lots of things that you can get started on, but every step of the way will need validation with performance data so we can find the very best way to do the work. Avoid rushing through the process and cutting corners. Avoid assuming there's a form you can do without. There isn't. In nonrepetitive work, we'll need to return to the work area whenever there is a particular task we are trying to understand. We need to be able to observe the work with an actual customer in real time to fully understand what happens and what should happen.

Special Event

You may find that you will need to hold a special event to gather and focus enough creative energy to get this process started. Put it on the calendar; make a detailed plan for who you need, what you need them to do, when and where you're going to start, and how you are going to continue by rolling through your workplace, step by step, to bring standardized work to everyone.

Capture the Current Way People Work

Use the standardized worksheet set provided at the end of this section to observe the work and capture all the timing data, material and information flows, motion patterns, and required equipment. Capture the current practice on video. As you study the current way people work, you are more likely to discover waste in the process steps. In nonrepetitive work environments, expect this to take weeks. The most important thing you'll discover in those nonrepetitive work environments is that many aspects of work are always repetitive, but the pace of that repetition could be very slow. In health care, patients may be unique, but the way we approach their handling and care should always be the same.

Build the Work Package

Carefully examine the work individuals do, taking advantage of the analysis offered by the worksheets. Build a package of tasks that three or four people can work together to complete. Create a better flow of information and materials by bringing the elements of work into one place, then focus on completing one item at a time, balancing the work so everyone is working at the same pace, and ensure everyone has the information, tools, and equipment to complete their work once they start. Support this work package by arranging the furniture, tools, printers, or other machines in a shape where the people working will be able to talk to each other as they work, and minimize the amount of time they are away from their work area. This four-step process for creating flow in a workplace (one place, one piece, one pace, one source) often leads to remarkable breakthroughs in productivity and worker satisfaction. We will discuss the work package in more detail in the section on standardized worksheets.

Find the Best Way

Once you decide where to start, you'll need to find a couple of people who are very good at doing the work you're trying to understand who are willing to work with you. These people form your pilot team. They will need to be the type of people who like to try new things and are excited about trying different ways to do the work. These people will help to decide what work goes into the work package and their goal is to find the very best way to finish the work package. As they conduct both structured and unstructured experiments with different ways to complete the work, they will find and capture the very best way. This experimentation phase may take weeks.

Graphics

Most people are highly visually oriented, so our standardized work needs to be built around pictures, drawings, or diagrams that make understanding each step easier. One of my favorite examples is an airline's seat-back safety card. It has very few words, so everyone can understand required evacuation processes regardless of their language skills. We want to make standardized work more graphical so people can see, perceive, and understand each step more quickly and more accurately than stopping to read a large chunk of text. Be careful with photographs, though, because they could potentially and unintentionally mislead the viewer. Often line drawings and diagrams, almost like comic books, will provide more direct and clear instructions. Your goal for the final standardized work product should be a highly graphical document.

Lock the Standard While Learning

Over the years, many people have learned about standardized work with Toyota as the primary example. They hear that Toyota's standardized work changes frequently, often daily, to accommodate team member improvements (kaizen). They conclude that standardized work has to change a lot. This is not true.

Standardized work is first and foremost a development tool for people's skills and thinking. Once the pilot team has defined the best way, you should lock the standardized work, allowing no additional changes until everyone responsible for doing that work has reached a level of expertise reflected by consistent attainment of that standard. When the team is performing to standard consistently, the team members will begin discussing new ways to do the work. If they don't, the leader may need to issue a new challenge to the team. That challenge may be to have them find a way to do the work more quickly (reduce the processing and/or cycle time), to reduce the floor space consumed by the work area, reduce the amount of material required to keep the workplace running, or reduce the number of people required to do the work. Remember to make goals specific and difficult, but not impossible. This maximizes the motivating potential of your challenge.

STANDARDIZED WORK WORKSHEET SET*

This section provides brief descriptions of the six primary standardized work worksheets used in the analysis and documentation of the work under review. For ANY work process, these forms can guide the analysis. I have collected a variety of worksheets over the years from a variety of sources. These represent cleaned up and consolidated versions of source documents that I use when teaching groups. They are flexible. They do not require an entry in each block on any form. Feel free to modify them to suit your needs.

I have presented them in the sequence below for convenience. The first four worksheets (standardized worksheet, time measurement sheet, combination table, and work balance chart) are for documenting and analyzing the current state. The last three worksheets (work balance chart, job breakdown sheet, and operation work standards sheet) are for designing and documenting the future state, or the work you intend to teach and do. For many tasks and jobs, people find it very easy to simply take the last two worksheets and write the steps they want to perform. For certain tasks, they are sufficient, especially if no instructions exist currently. However, these are not analytical forms. They provide enough information to perform the task and monitor performance, but changes will require the analytical part as well.

Standardized Work Chart

Use this chart (Figure 8.1) for a line drawing of the work area under analysis, and work up the initial set of work steps, recorded under "operation elements." Leave timing information blank until the time measurement sheet is complete.

---

* For Adobe PDF and Microsoft Excel versions of these sheets, download from our website at www. leadersights.com

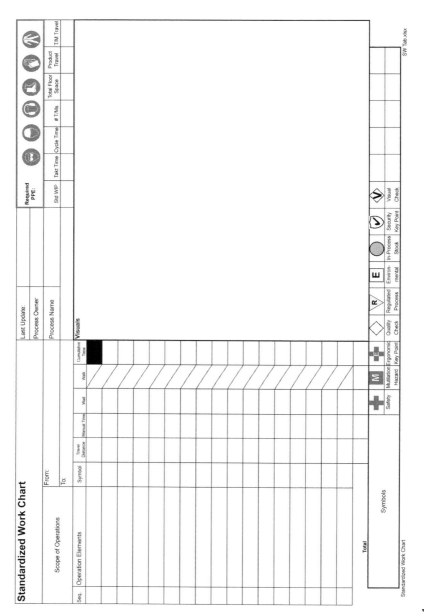

FIGURE 8.1
Standardized work chart.

Time Measurement Worksheet

This worksheet (Figure 8.2) allows you to capture the time it takes an individual to perform the required set of tasks. The tasks should be the same as those on the standardized work chart. There are columns for 17 observations of this performance. Good decisions require at least four observations. Better decisions result from more observations. For repetitive work, you may be able to capture many of these observations in a single day, but don't. Always complete this worksheet over several different days when a larger variety of environmental factors will come into play in affecting the performance of the work. For nonrepetitive tasks, it may take several weeks to capture enough data to make better decisions. Use separate sheets for separate people, and always remind them to do the work the best way they know how and to do it the same way every time.

After gathering the observations, don't forget to decide on the charted time for each operation element. This is rarely just an average of the observations. The charted time should be the time that is most likely to occur. Some people use the mode. Others will throw out the highest and lowest and calculate an average of the rest. Give this some thought, decide, record the charted time then transfer the charted times to the standardized work chart.

Combination Table

The combination table (Figure 8.3) is likely to be the most helpful, but is probably the most misunderstood of the forms in the set. It begins with the same set of operation elements as the previous two worksheets, as well as the charted times from the time measurement sheet. Then, graphically portray the charted times as bars that extend across the grid the appropriate length to reflect the actual time consumed. Then discuss and decide if the element just plotted is value-added, nonvalue added but still necessary, or nonvalue added and unnecessary. Use colors to make the different categories stand out (green for value-added and red for nonvalue-added.) Each element's bar will begin where the previous one ended. Post this chart in the work area in order to remind everyone to think of ways to remove the red and reduce the whole thing. Unlike the time measurement sheet, you can combine multiple people on this chart (hence the name.) You can

Time Measurement Worksheet

Operator: ________ Shift: ______ Date: ______ Recorded by: ________

Scope of Operation: From: To:

Seq. No.	Operation Elements	Starting Point	1	2	3	4	5	6	7	8	9	10	11	12	13	14	15	16	17	Charted times	Remarks
	Cycle Time (totals)																				

Use digital watch or stopwatch and record elements to nearest 0.1 second. Scan each row and, rounding to nearest second, specify "most repeatable" time to be the "Charted Time".

Time Measurement Worksheet SW Tab.xlsx

FIGURE 8.2
Time measurement worksheet.

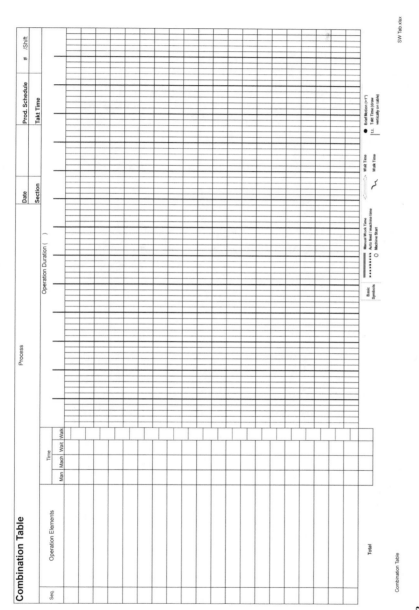

FIGURE 8.3

Combination table.

highlight the handoffs between people as we try to get work completed through the cycle.

Work Balance Chart

The work balance chart allows you to show the amount of work that each person in a focus area is doing, and how much is value added and non-value added. Building from the combination table, stack the operation elements for each person in a single process column. Add the work others do and compare how much time each consumes. It will be easy to see how someone may be overburdened or under-burdened. See Figures 8.4 and 8.5 for an example.

Job Breakdown Sheet

Use this form (Figure 8.6) to describe the new work that each team member does as a result of changing the work elements around on the work balance chart. Identify the key points of each step, and explain why they are key steps.

Operation Work Standards Sheet

This form (Figure 8.7) becomes the primary training tool and quick reference tool available in the workplace. It will include new operation elements from the job breakdown sheet and all the pictures necessary to do the assigned work. Avoid the temptation to use multiple pages. If the work is so complex that it needs multiple pages, then go simplify the work first! Examine a smaller period of time, or a smaller work space if necessary.

Use lots of simple diagrams and drawings to highlight the key points of the work. You may choose to laminate this final version and post it in the workspace so people can refer to it if they have a discrepancy in how they performed a task, or if they have an idea to improve the work. You should encourage people to put notes right on the form and discuss in their teams when they might be able to test the new ideas to see if they are actually better. If they are, then you need to provide a support person to help the team document the new way and update the standardized work.

This will also be the primary worksheet for leader standardized work (LSW) presented on pages 163–169.

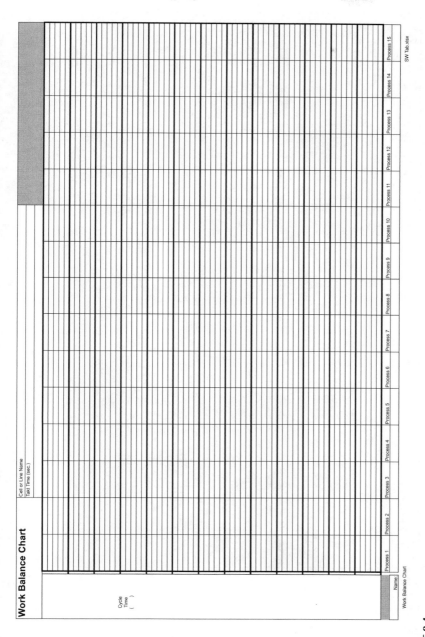

FIGURE 8.4
Work balance chart.

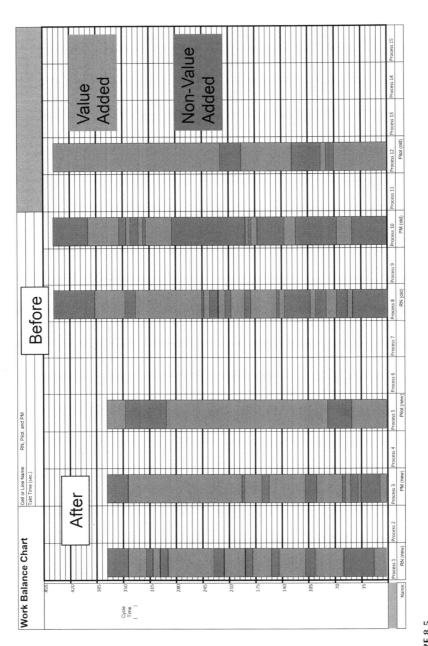

FIGURE 8.5
Work balance chart example.

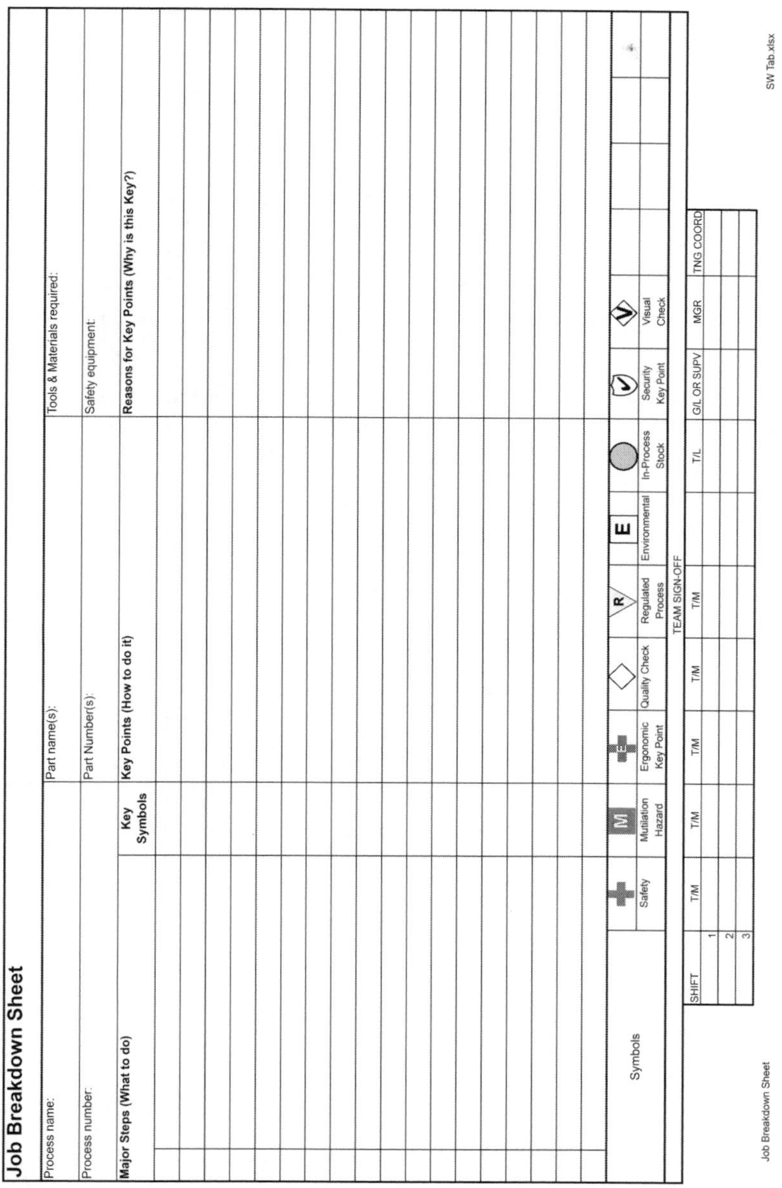

FIGURE 8.6
Job breakdown sheet.

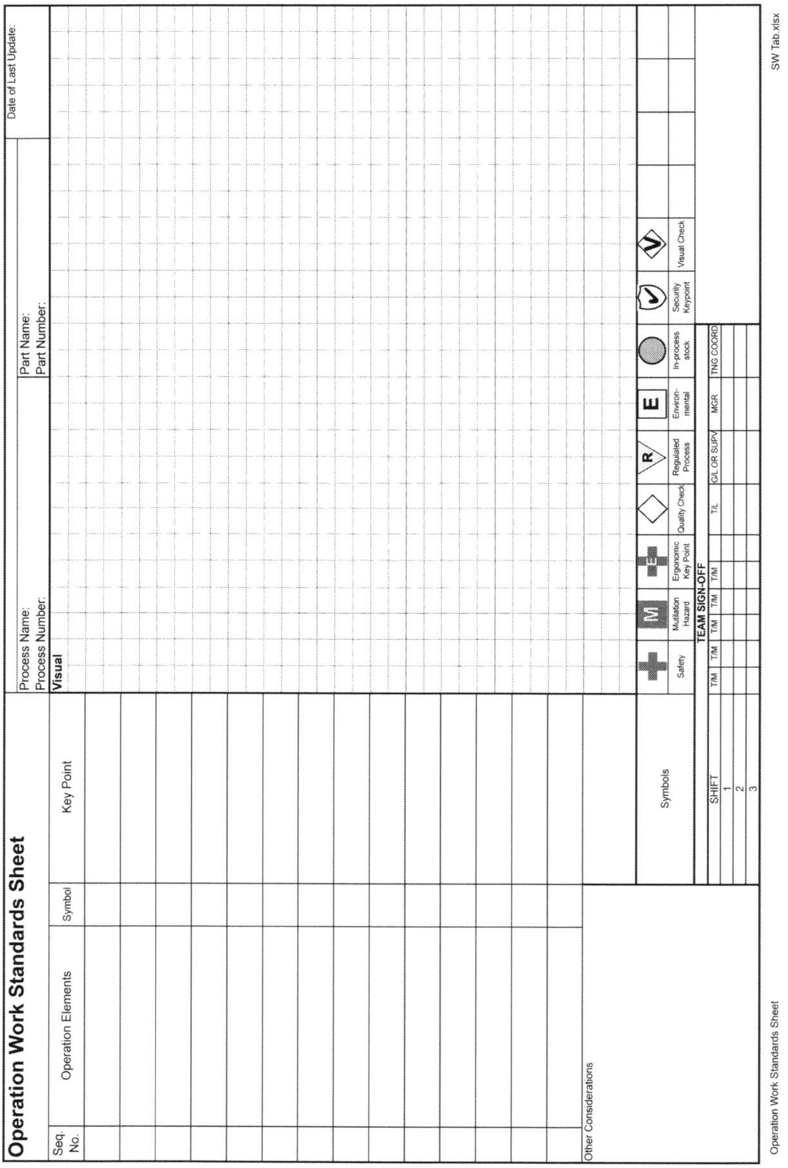

Operation Work Standards Sheet

Process Name: ___ Part Name: ___ Date of Last Update: ___
Process Number: ___ Part Number: ___

Seq. No.	Operation Elements	Symbol	Key Point	Visual

Other Considerations

Symbols

| ✚ Safety | M Mutilation Hazard | ✚ Ergonomic Key Point | ◇ Quality Check | R Regulated Process | E Environ-mental | ● In-process stock | ↩ Security Keypoint | ◇ Visual Check |

TEAM SIGN-OFF

SHIFT	T/M	T/M	T/M	T/M	T/M	T/L	GL OR SUPV	MGR	TNG COORD
1									
2									
3									

Operation Work Standards Sheet

SW Tab.xlsx

FIGURE 8.7
Operation work standards sheet.

THE WORK PACKAGE

The key functions of a work package include the following:

- Promoting systems thinking by tying several functions together toward a more finished product or service (wholeness brings significance as it ties work more closely to the customer).
- Building higher skills in a variety of tasks and functions to offer personal growth, job security, and higher self-efficacy.
- Offering ownership to the team of the work and the output of the work.
- Gaining more employee satisfaction by emphasizing the importance of the individual's role in the system, offering a variety of tasks or activities in the course of a day's work, increasing the team's awareness of what others are doing, and delivering additional responsibility without increasing the individual work burden of any team member.

Work Package for Repetitive Work

Let me illustrate the process of creating a work package with this simple example from a simulation my colleague Jon Yingling created and that I often use in workshops.

The output of our simulated work system consists of two "products." The first product is a set of two 3 × 5 index cards, each with a different letter written on it, assembled and aligned, then stapled with the staples folded in. The second product is the same, except with different letters and/or colors and with the staples folded out (just to simulate different customer requirements). At the Ohio State University, we use the letters O and H in red ink on the first product and the letters I and O in black ink on the second. I should note that we have used a variety of letters to try to connect with our audiences wherever we use this. We used AC and CM in Australia, for the Adelaide Crows and the Collingwood Magpies of the Australian Football League, for example. For simplicity, I'll use OH and IO for the remainder of this illustration.

In the baseline round, which simulates the current way most work systems operate, we create departments for each function. The first completes the O writing, with two operators, one with a red pen and one with a black pen. There is an I-writing department and an H-writing department as well. Each department receives blank cards from a paper supplier in batches of five and writes their assigned letter on the cards as quickly as possible, then calls for a courier to transport the cards to the next process. As soon as the courier takes the cards, the writers can write another batch.

The next process is assembly, where one operator takes a card from the red O stack and aligns it on top of a card from the red H stack, securing it with a paper clip. A second operator does the same with the black O and I. When a batch of 5 is complete, a courier takes the batch to the next process: stapling. Stapling finishes each set by checking the alignment, stapling each set in the top left corner, then removing the paper clip. The stapling team then changes the settings on the stapler for the next set of cards (remember, one folds them in, the other folds them out). Couriers take batches of 5 finished goods to the accountant, where they are counted as shipped complete.

On the surface, this sounds like an assembly simulation where a manufacturing company is making a product for sale, with fabrication and assembly work stations and equipment, and transferring materials and inventory from place to place within a factory using forklifts. Many people who work in administrative or transactional services operations are skeptical of its value until we remind them that the products are simply documents or reports with a required set of data (the letters) that must be properly formatted and assembled (clipping) then approved for release (stapling) to an internal or external customer. These could be travel claims, sales reports, medical charts, marketing collateral, purchase orders, shipping receipts, patient transfer requests, dispatch orders, insurance policy change orders, deposit slips for bank accounts, stock trade orders, or anything else that requires data to be organized into a more useful format for someone else.

The departments responsible for the work are scattered throughout the workplace. In reality, this represents different departments within an organization, whether they are within the same campus or business park, or located in different cities around the globe.

Because each department is scattered throughout the workplace, transferring the product from place to place takes significant effort and delays the delivery of the final product even if the mode of transfer is electronic.

Documenting the standardized work for any single department simply captures the way that individual group works, independent of the others. The work is isolated. The workers don't feel any connection to the larger product or organization, much less the customer. The future state for this work may not change the specific tasks that any one person does, but we need to change the work environment to enrich and enhance the employee experience. The work package will do that.

We start by mapping the value stream for these products. This will not only identify clearly the steps required to finish the product, in the proper sequence, and the time each takes, but also capture the delays, the transfers, and the backlogs that slow the system. Then, we analyze to see what work we can do in one particular place. If we focus on the customer, we will be able to see that if we take the red O writer from the O-writing department, and put him at a table with the red H writer, then take the person from the clipping department who assembled the OH product and create space for him at the table, we have a pretty nice work package of three functions, each separate, but now linked to the other work steps required to finish the product with the exception of stapling. We'll do the same with the black O writer, the black I writer, and the I-O clipper in a separate cell.

Unfortunately, at this stage, we can't integrate stapling into the cell because there is only one stapler and two different products. We can, however, move those cells much closer to the stapling department, perhaps even so close that we need not accumulate inventory between the two.

As we look at preparing the standardized work, the work package now contains an O-writing task, an H-writing task, and an assembly task that we link together with a set of kanban spaces to regulate the work flow. We can assign a fourth team member to fill a team leader role and we have a physical structure that promotes teamwork, provides visibility of the nearly finished product to the team and aligns with specific customers, allows for rotation among the team members through those different work tasks, and provides accountability and responsibility for the product. We'll create a work package for another team centered on stapling as well, perhaps integrating a quality function or shipping. In your work environment, how can you break up certain existing departments and organize to support a set of customers? How can you link steps of work together so that a set of people working together can learn from each other with every work cycle?

Work Package for Non-Repetitive Work

In a manufacturing job shop, or in sales offices, design and project management firms, law offices, schools, hospitals and clinics, retail, government, supply chain management, or any other work that doesn't require people to do the same set of tasks within a regular time interval all through the day, standardized work is often a hard sell. But consider this: all work is repetitive. Maybe it isn't repetitive like a factory making cars with one coming off the end of the line every 53 seconds, but if you think about what you were hired to do, there are several tasks of varying difficulty performed at irregular time intervals. If a patient comes into an emergency department regardless of their condition, there is a pattern to their diagnosis and treatment response. Sometimes they have a rash. Sometimes they have respiratory distress. Sometimes they've been in a horrific accident. The pattern of response is the same, but the urgency varies. I don't want to downplay the significance of what these dedicated people do, but if there weren't patterns, we couldn't teach things in medical or nursing school.

What are the skills that we want to improve for these people? That's the leader's job to figure out. In these environments where the complexity of the work we have to do is highly variable, we need to ensure that we have standardized work for the various tasks, and wherever we can, we assemble sets of these tasks into a day-long work package and do what we can to level load the work among a team of people. Again, this begins with understanding the value stream and building task- and skill-oriented standardized work. If a patient requires intubation, there is standardized work for that. If a new project requires research for material sourcing, there is standardized work for that.

By grouping projects, patients, or customers into categorical sets based on variability and complexity, then defining and building standardized work for the most commonly required tasks, and we manage these as they arrive in our workplace so that we don't constantly assign the easiest work to one person and the hardest to another, we have a pretty good work package that we can even practice for.

Another challenge for nonrepetitive work is variability in demand. Some days are busy and some are slow. On busy days, there are routine tasks that go undone, and most of the time, that's okay. But in those stretches of several busy days back to back, and those routine tasks include replenishing supplies, cleaning up, reorganizing, and problem solving, we could end up in trouble very soon. The work package we build will allow us to flex the work schedule so that even during busy stretches, we will be able to have someone focus on the routine things, while others fight the battle, knowing that when it comes time to rotate, everyone in the battle will get a chance to work on something a little different, without just disconnecting.

The package of tasks, together with a carefully constructed rotation schedule, provides everyone with variety of tasks to do during the day, ensures everything gets done as needed, reduces the likelihood of employee burn-out, and gives the team additional feelings of responsibility. Everyone still has a hand in completing the "main" work, which will address their need for significance, and if we keep everything posted on a visual management system board in the team's work area (Chapter 7), they will constantly be aware of the standards for safety, quality, schedule attainment, cost, and any other key metric we decide to focus on. Together, even when the workday is busy, it stays well organized and packaged, and everyone can be satisfied at the end of the day, know exactly how they contributed to success; and it is hard to beat that feeling of accomplishment, knowing that the day was crazy, but we made it through even better than we thought we could.

LEADER STANDARDIZED WORK

We conduct a rigorous analysis when developing standardized work for our people. We use the standardized work as the basis of a Training-Within-Industry (TWI) approach to teach operators up to a level of expertise that allows them to work without constant referral to the standardized work documents. This has proven to be highly effective.

The literature available on LSW usually focuses on creating checklists of the activities required during a certain interval of time; usually daily and weekly checks. The leader is required to refer to the checklist rigidly (think pilots in preflight or during emergency procedures), preventing mistakes of omission and building a regular habit of interacting with the workforce. In most cases though, the checklist requires leaders to simply check the work of others (*check*-list), which is a form of an audit or inspection. Our lean philosophy tells us that, if people are routinely doing quality work, then checking their work is not adding any value, therefore the leader's inspection is waste. Why then would we just want leaders to do this nonvalue-adding, functionary, block-checking BS and call it standardized work? Let us rethink this approach.

I want to be clear—leaders need to check things. I'm not disputing that. But the true goal of standardized work is to develop expertise and self-efficacy; therefore, the purpose of LSW should be the same. We want to cultivate positive patterns of behavior in our leaders. I don't think we can get that with a simple checklist of things to do. Leaders also have an obligation to set the proper behavioral example for the workforce. If we expect everyone else to strictly follow standardized work, we should be following standardized work ourselves. In essence, developing leaders through the use of standardized work is the same as developing skills in other team members through standardized work, so making a special designation of "leader's" standardized work may not be necessary. After all, we will ideally be making leaders from all our team members, with certain expectations for certain behaviors. For now, though, I will continue to use LSW to describe the standardized work we create in order to build leadership skills and cultivate proper leader behaviors.

Leaders typically perform regular tasks at irregular intervals, so the guidelines for nonrepetitive work packages also apply to LSW. As with other types of standardized work, we want LSW to be as repetitive as possible to ensure we build skill on an ongoing basis.

We want to use standardized work to build skills of leadership, so we first have to define what those skills are and how they appear in our behavior. In Chapter 6, we pointed out the following leader behaviors in the integral leadership model:

- Loving, with behaviors that reflect coaching skills: challenging, supporting, correcting, and encouraging (zone 1 behaviors)
- Learning, with behaviors that reflect humility and focus on succession, or teaching and developing subordinate leaders with behaviors related to curiosity, questioning, and listening (zone 2 behaviors)
- Letting go, with behaviors related to goal setting, rewarding experimental efforts, encouraging, and short-interval contact (zone 3 behaviors)

- Connecting, with behaviors related to attracting new talent and new opportunities, sharing successes and overcoming failures, and showing confidence and certainty (zone 4 behaviors)

I can't say that I have all of this figured out yet, so I'm counting on your help. Earlier, I described building a nonrepetitive work package by aggregating sets of standardized work for discrete tasks and arranging them throughout the day to build a full work day. Each task should have clear definition of major steps, key points in each, and reasons why they are important (see the job breakdown sheet in the standardized work set). Each task should also have an expected duration, setting a clear expectation that they should be completed within a certain time limit. When we deviate from that time limit, we have to explore why to discover problems that may not always be obvious. These behaviors are often similar and related to each other, so there won't be a one-to-one task-to-behavior approach. Instead, in the LSW we create, we'll need to identify the primary targeted behavior, as well as others we can affect.

The base set of standardized work to develop proper integral leader behaviors described above might include the following:

- LSW for encouraging (see an example in Figures 8.8 and 8.9)
- LSW for goal setting and challenging current performance
- LSW for scheduled listening time
- LSW for correcting wrong performance and behavior
- LSW for in process teaching and coaching
- LSW for short-interval checking
  - LSW for system gemba walk
  - LSW for process gemba walk
  - LSW for problem-solving gemba walk
- LSW for connecting and attracting

Each of these will have a job breakdown sheet and a one-page lesson (or an operation work standards sheet) for reference and for teaching. Leaders may choose to post these where they will have reminders throughout their workplace.

We will need to build a cadence matrix to ensure we cycle through all of these at regular intervals. It might look like Figure 8.10. These will then be organized on the leader's calendar or diary in a sequence perhaps like Figure 8.11.

Title	LSW_Encouraging	Purpose	To help leaders build better relationships with people in the workplace
Frequency	Daily—Multiple	Desired Outcome	Build trust in the workplace for more effective communication of requirements, feedback, problems, and ideas
Effective Date	April 30, 2016	Review cadence	Monthly: Second Friday after standup meeting

Encourage	Major Steps	Target Duration	Key Points	Reasons Why
1	Notice the need for encouragement	<1 minute	They aren't achieving their goals; They are not themselves as you know them to be; They seem distracted or sad	Ongoing discouragement can lead people to mistakes on the job, or may prevent them from reporting a discovered problem, or prevent them from submitting an improvement idea
2	Initiate the conversation	1–4 minutes	Ask them a friendly but open-ended question that will require a thoughtful response. "Hi, Bob. Can you tell me how things are working well or not for you today?' Avoid pointing out a failure or how they may look	You will need to understand what they are reacting to so you can properly encourage them
3	Listen	2–10 minutes	Give them your undivided attention. Do not interrupt. Do not criticize or judge. Just listen	Shows you respect their time, feelings, and contributions
4	Affirm	1–4 minutes	Let them know you've heard them and understand Remind them of the value they bring to the workplace, citing a specific strength or past success	This will help them to remember that they have been successful before and they can do it again
5	Offer perspective	1–4 minutes	If they have focused on negative outcomes or constraints in the workplace, offer a view of the positive they can consider. Avoid giving advice or solutions Simply share a different perspective	This will reduce the likelihood that they will continue on a negative trend toward depression and perhaps give them hope for the future
6	Offer Support	1–4 minutes	Rather than tell them what they should do or what you can do for them, ask them how you can best support them in their efforts	Having them focus on how you can help will reduce the likelihood that they will view your suggestions as judgmental or critical
7	Return to reconnect with them later in the day	2–4 hours		

File name:	LSW_Enc.xlsx	Owner: HRD/Carol Evans	Last review: 8 April 2016

FIGURE 8.8

LSW for encouraging—Job breakdown sheet.

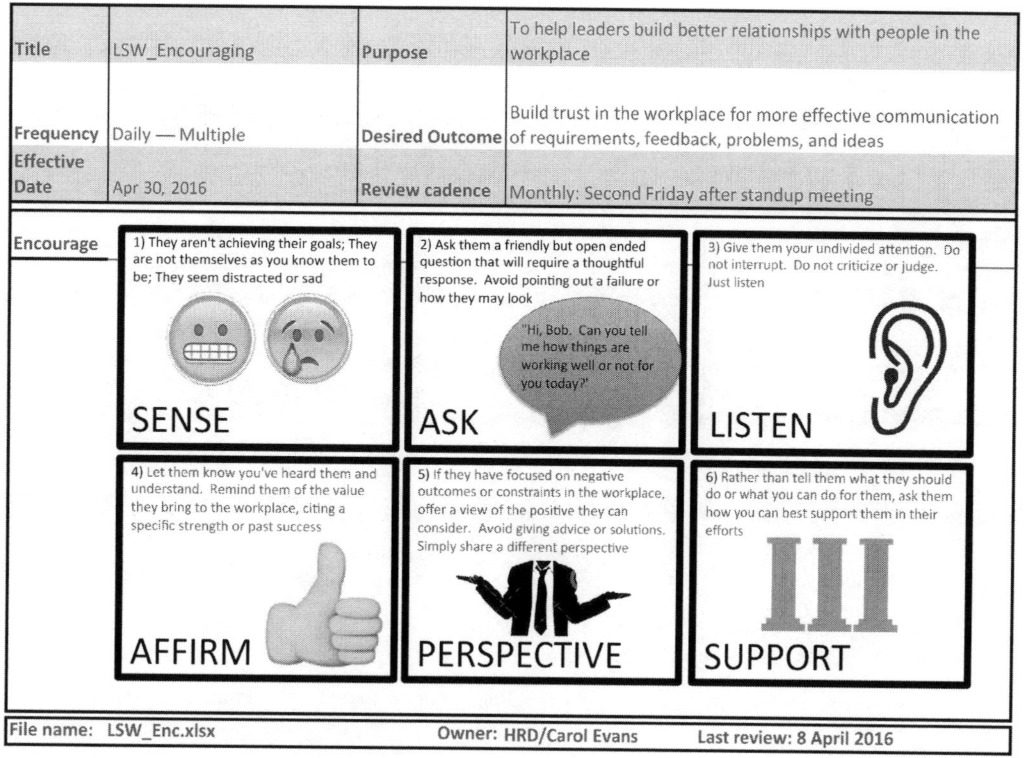
Title
LSW_Encouraging
Purpose
To help leaders build better relationships with people in the workplace
Frequency
Daily — Multiple
Desired Outcome
Build trust in the workplace for more effective communication of requirements, feedback, problems, and ideas
Effective Date
Apr 30, 2016
Review cadence
Monthly: Second Friday after standup meeting
Encourage
1) They aren't achieving their goals; They are not themselves as you know them to be; They seem distracted or sad
SENSE
2) Ask them a friendly but open ended question that will require a thoughtful response. Avoid pointing out a failure or how they may look
"Hi, Bob. Can you tell me how things are working well or not for you today?"
ASK
3) Give them your undivided attention. Do not interrupt. Do not criticize or judge. Just listen
LISTEN
4) Let them know you've heard them and understand. Remind them of the value they bring to the workplace, citing a specific strength or past success
AFFIRM
5) If they have focused on negative outcomes or constraints in the workplace, offer a view of the positive they can consider. Avoid giving advice or solutions. Simply share a different perspective
PERSPECTIVE
6) Rather than tell them what they should do or what you can do for them, ask them how you can best support them in their efforts
SUPPORT
File name: LSW_Enc.xlsx
Owner: HRD/Carol Evans
Last review: 8 April 2016

FIGURE 8.9
LSW for encouraging—Operation work standards sheet.

Frequency	SW Element	Owner	Targeted Skills/Behavior	Desired Outcomes	Review Cycle
Daily					
	Encouraging	Bea Apier	E; H; SP; L	Make contact and talk to every team member every day	M
	Teaching and Coaching	Warren Peace	T: L; Q	Build thinking and doing skills	
	Correcting	Ann Thracks	CO; CH; H; Q	Ensure proper techniques	
	Short-Interval Checking	Ima Walker	CH; GS; CF; Q	Understand what's going on in the business, know where to provide additional resources	
1x	Process gemba walk	Howard I. Know	L; CU; R	Be present and useful	
2x	Problem solving gemba walk				
	Attend Team Huddle (rotating)				
	Administration	Chris Anthemum	GS; CE; H; SP	Stay on top of things	
2-3 x/week					
	Scheduled Listening Time	Eileen Dover	L; SP; E; H	Build better relationships	Q
	Customer relationship mgt	May Flowers	CF; CE; SP	Build better relationships	
Weekly					
	Goal Setting/Challenging	Ken Eiguther	GS; CH; R; CF	Achieve higher performance levels	M/Q/A
	Short-Interval Checking	Ben Rundabit	CH;GS; CF; R; Q	Understand interactions between organizational units	Q
	System gemba walk				
Monthly					
	Connecting and Attracting	Sarah Tonin	CE; CF; L; SP	Attract and retain the best talent	Q/A

Behavior Codes:	Humility (H)	Encouraging (E)	Listening (L)
	Challenging(CH)	Teaching/Developing (T)	Goal Setting (GS)
	Supporting (SP)	Curiosity (CU)	Rewarding (R)
	Correcting (CO)	Questioning (Q)	Showing Confidence (CF)
			Showing Certainty (CE)

FIGURE 8.10
LSW cadence calendar.

Title	LSW Daily Schedule		Purpose	To help leaders manage their time and lead their people.
Frequency	Daily - Multiple		Desired Outcome	All required tasks are completed
Effective Date	April 30, 2016		Review cadence	Weekly
Hour	Event		Reference	Notes (What did you discover today?)
6:00 – 6:45	Short Interval Checking (System walk through — Bird's Eye View)		LSW_SICSys	
6:45 – 7:00	Buffer/Correcting/Coaching		LSW_CO	
7:00 – 7:15	Huddle at Team 1 Board		SW_TmHuddle	
7:15 – 8:45	Short Interval Checking (Process walk through — Fish's Eye View)		LSW_SICProcess	
8:45 – 9:00	Buffer/Correcting/Coaching		LSW_CO	
9:00 – 9:30	Meeting at Group 2 Board (LSW Connecting)		SW_GroupHuddle	
9:30 – 10:00	Buffer/Disseminate Info/Problem Solving			
10:00 – 11:00	Admin — Email/phone/calendar management			
11:00 – 12:00	Lunch with Team 3 (LSW Encouraging/LSW Scheduled Listening)		LSW_E:LSW_SL	
12:00 – 1:45	Short Interval Checking (Problem Solving — Insect's Eye View) (LSW In-Process Teaching)		LSW_SICProb	
1:45 – 2:00	Buffer/Correcting/Coaching		LSW_CO	
2:00 – 2:45	Planning next 2 days schedule (LSW Goal Setting)		LSW_DS	
2:45 – 3:00	Short Interval Checking (LSW Goal Setting and Challenging)		LSW_GS;CH:SICSys	
File name:	LSW_DS.xlsx			Owner: Dwayne Hisgob

FIGURE 8.11
LSW daily schedule.

SIMPLE CIRCLE EVALUATION

To ensure we cycle through all the necessary actions to develop key leader skills, there needs to be a regular feedback system. For years, we've had access to 360° evaluation instruments. Many workplaces use these either annually or biannually in order to provide feedback to leaders from their leaders, peers, and their people.

The first time a leader undergoes one of these can be terrifying; because when fear of retribution is out of the picture, people will tell you what they really think. But it is very difficult for us to assess our own behavior with accuracy, so the 360° assessment is an excellent tool for development and should be used regularly. My colleagues in Australia have worked the Human Synergistics Model Circumplex into their graduate certificate programs, giving participants a chance to complete team evaluations and, occasionally, the full spectrum evaluation that really opens eyes for individuals, teams, and the organization as a whole. I think these kinds of assessment instruments are very helpful in measuring behavioral and cultural things where often there is no way to do so. I want to submit a more frequent and more immediate type of feedback for you to ponder, though.

Building mastery in any skill requires unbiased feedback from a perspective other than your own. To induce a state of psychological flow (or to get "in the zone"), an activity must provide immediate performance feedback (Csikszentmihalyi, 1990). I've seen several workplaces with daily morale checks on their visual boards, and the simple circle evaluation I envision flows from those.

The objectives of the simple circle system are for workplaces:

1. To regularly assess and provide feedback transparently to leaders at all levels regarding their consistent satisfaction of behaviors reflecting the workplace's values
2. To drive self-reflection and development of leadership skills
3. To engage employees in improving the quality of leadership
4. To create trust in a workplace through a forum that openly addresses how leaders do their work and how others perceive leader behavior

In the example I've provided in Figure 8.12, I've listed 13 behaviors. Each of these will have standardized work like the example for encouragement

Leader's Name		Leader's Role			In Role Since			
Targeted Skills/Behavior		Simple Circle Scoring						Specific Action Plans
	W1	W2	W3	W4	Best	Needs Work	YTD	
Humility	●				●		△	
Challenging	◎						◆	
Supporting	△					▽	▼	
Correcting		✖				✖	▼	3 Gemba Walks with
Encouraging		◎					△	Bob
Teaching/Developing		◎					△	
Curiosity			△				▽	Moonshine rotation in
Questioning			◎				▼	July
Listening			✖				▼	3 Gemba Walks with
GoalSetting				●	●		△	Bob
Rewarding				◎			▲	
Showing Confidence				△			△	
Showing Certainty				◎			▲	

Simple Circle Eval						
1	2	3	4	5	6	7
Needs Work			OK			Crushing it

FIGURE 8.12
LSW simple circle example.

provided earlier, so everyone in the workplace should know what the expected behavior is. Once a week, everyone—team members, the leader, peer leaders, and senior leaders—will submit their scores for the leader in three or four categories by simply assigning points to each. The score for each category will range from 1 to 7 points, with 1 meaning "needs work," 4 meaning "OK," and 7 meaning "Crushing It" or words to that effect (yes, choose your own!). Everyone will also identify which behaviors the leader best exhibits, and the ones in which he or she needs more focused work.

Each week will focus on a different set of targeted behaviors so that all 13 will be covered over the month. Team members may do their assessments at the end of a daily huddle and can simply put their individual scores on the whiteboard. Subordinate leaders, peer leaders, and senior leaders will add theirs to the whiteboards for other leaders during their gemba walks that day. The individual leaders themselves will average the scores for each behavior before placing the appropriate red X, green O, or yellow triangle for each. The direction of the triangles should reflect the trend from the previous rating, and in the year to date (YTD) column, all should record the trends from month to month. Anything rated an average of 4 or less and trending down should have a specific action plan to try to correct the behavior.

I suppose we could make this a cumbersome, data-driven exercise. We could record all the individual scores in a database, analyze trends over months and months, and use these details in data-driven annual performance appraisals. If this isn't very simple though, it will never last long. That's why I recommend doing everything directly on the whiteboard with the rest of the visuals. Senior leaders have to make a point of using the colors as points for coaching and celebration rather than brutally focusing on weaknesses, and of course the way those senior leaders handle these issues will reflect on their own leaderboards too.

CHAPTER SUMMARY

Standardized work is the single most important system in the continuous improvement world.

The greatest value in standardized work is ultimately in the freedom of the people doing the work to see and solve problems in their work package, find better ways to do the work, test them, implement them as a new standard, and teach other team members how to do the work the new way.

The critical success factor is designing new work packages, documenting that new way to work, and teaching the workforce how the new work process works. Don't just document the way you're doing the work; use detailed analysis and understanding to create new and better work for everyone in the workplace.

The standardized work philosophy flows from a lean philosophy that is people-oriented; one that drives success by constantly creating greater value.

We have three equal goals in our workplace philosophy: higher productivity, higher profitability, and higher professionalism. Professionalism is the most difficult because the other two have often threatened employees in their implementation.

The key purpose of standardized work is to develop people by building cognitive and technical skills, creating a just and equitable workplace, and creating a satisfying workplace. Together, these can change the culture of any organization.

The five goals of standardized work (per Yingling and Damodaraswamy) are

- Make tacit knowledge explicit
- Build in control
- Focus on methodology
- Simplify
- Go beyond skill

Understanding the work, and redesigning it into effective work packages is a difficult and time-consuming task but mustn't be rushed through shortcuts.

Use the standardized work chart, the time measurement worksheet, the combination table, and the work balance chart to understand the work in a particular workspace. Use these to complete the analysis that will lead to understanding.

Use the work balance chart, job breakdown sheet, and operation work standards sheet to design the new work packages and document how the new work must be done.

The work package is the key to people development, and to creating work that is highly productive with high quality, as well as personally and professionally satisfying to everyone. This is true for both repetitive and nonrepetitive work.

LSW should accomplish the same thing for leaders as regular standardized work accomplishes for others—developing people; in this case, developing the kinds of leaders that we want in our workplaces.

LSW goes beyond a checklist and into building the real behaviors we want in leaders: loving, learning, and letting go.

The simple circle evaluation is a way to provide effective feedback to leaders from their leaders, peers, and their people. It should also serve to build trust in a workplace.

9

A Rigorous Learning Suggestion System

Suggestion programs, systems, and schemes have been a part of workplace cultures since the 1890s. None are flawless, some are excellent, and many are horrible, despite being introduced with the best of intentions. To support ongoing development of our people, workplaces need a suggestion system that contributes to that learning goal, as well as to the improved performance of the collective workplace.

Learning means developing cognitive skills or brainpower. To build a learning environment that really develops people, leaders will need to establish personal relationships with their people. Like all personal relationships, the quality and value of the relationship to each person depends on the level of trust between the two of them.

Few leaders are given practical tools to help build that trust to a higher level. Many are never taught how to actually discuss things with others or how to specifically interact with people in order to solicit trust. This deficit may be especially pronounced in fields where expertise takes years to develop, and the consequences of failure are very high (medicine, engineering, and aviation). Believe it or not, many of the barriers to trust we commonly face can be overcome with a modified suggestion system, designed and built with the right purpose and outcomes in mind.

A proper suggestion system provides a standard process that people can use to solve problems. Sometimes, the suggestions people make highlight problems. Most suggestions though, are desired solutions to unstated problems. In either case, the system needs to require that leaders help people think through their problem or idea. The suggestion system must provide a platform for repetition and a reinforcement of critical thinking and performance, thus teaching people how to work deliberately through their submission and ensure that individual and collective performance improves over time. When we overlay effective coaching and disciplined adherence to the process, this system is robust and rigorous.

In this chapter, we'll describe how the suggestion system I have in mind not only addresses trust, but also provides a structure that can lead to a new culture of learning and continuous improvement in the workplace.

BREAK THE SUGGESTION BOX

The suggestion box symbolizes many of the features of the workplace culture:

- It is placed in a spot where everyone can see it and it is known that the leaders in the workplace are willing to hear from their employees.
- It is usually locked, perhaps because we don't trust each other enough not to steal our great idea.
- It emphasizes that "smart" people will review and evaluate all of your ideas, and judge whether or not they are worthy of further consideration.

Many people I talk to realize that the suggestion box is quickly fading as a working tool in workplaces, and I want to accelerate that demise. I tell people who still have a suggestion box hanging on a wall to go and remove it immediately, preferably with a big hammer. I have had one company president who liked his "suggestion" box simply because he was personally responsible for it. He viewed it as a direct line for his people to share their concerns with him. I can't disagree with that thinking, but I can't label it as a suggestion system either. If the purpose of the tool is to give your workforce an anonymous channel to say things to you, then go for it, but that's not going to do what we need a suggestion system to do.

In the suggestion systems I've studied over the years, whether with a suggestion box or not, the intended purposes all sound similar: to promote employee engagement, to give employees a voice, to capture the great ideas of our work force, etc.; all very noble. I summarize these goals in one term: idea mining. We know that there's gold in those hills (or ideas in those employees). If we can just dig a little at them, or squeeze them a little bit, those ideas will start flowing, and we can decide whether they're any good or not. The digging and squeezing doesn't necessarily have to be mean-spirited, but with all of these systems, managers are trying to compel employees to give their ideas to the organization, usually with only a token reward for them. If we're going to promote learning, loving, and letting go, these systems need to give something to the employees instead of taking something from them. We really need to rethink the purpose of the system.

The purpose of the system should align with the values of the workplace, and its goals of becoming a learning organization. Therefore, we need a system whose primary purpose is to teach a set of skills to the workforce, skills they can use at work as well as in their private lives. The most important of these skills for the workforce are critical thinking, quantitative analysis, creativity, planning and organizing, execution, and evaluation. On top of all of these, leaders also need to be able to build trusting relationships and learn how to properly interact with people throughout the workplace. I designed the C4 process to do all of these.

THE C4 PROCESS

In 2011, we published "The C4 Process: Four Vital Steps to Better Work." As a basic problem-solving process, it is what I consider an improved version of the Shewhart/Deming plan–do–check–act (PDCA) cycle. C4 is short for concern–cause–countermeasure–confirm. Anecdotally, those I have shared it with have found it easier to follow than Toyota's A3 process based on PDCA. I would like to say that it led to better results too, but I haven't done a deliberate and unbiased comparative study to make that claim. I can say, however, that after teaching PDCA for years, I have gotten better learning results from groups, and more enthusiasm from participants, since I started teaching C4.

The C4 book focuses primarily on teams using the C4 process to solve significant problems in their workplace and using an A3-sized C4 worksheet to document their progress and anticipate the subsequent steps of the process. With the C4 suggestion system, I want to focus on building meaningful relationships within the workplace, and driving more rigorous learning processes for individuals. Chapter 7 of *The C4 Process* describes how to use C4 cards to surface problems and ideas, and use a C4 board to keep track of them, all integrated into the visual management system. The following section is a reprint of that chapter with a few minor adjustments or corrections. Afterwards, we will share some additional ideas about making this learning system even more effective.

Chapter 7—Managing the C4 Process: Engaging Everyone

The C4 worksheet is a powerful way to initiate the C4 process within a work area, but it can be somewhat intimidating when first introduced (see Figure 9.1). For problems that don't require this level of comprehensive detail, the C4 card condenses the problem-solving structure so that individual employees can use it alongside coaching support.

Making the C4 process accessible and useful to everyone in the organization provides a channel to higher levels of employee involvement and engagement. The card gives employees a little more control over their work and their workplace. Like the C4 worksheet, the card guides employees through the problem-solving process while simultaneously building their skills in analysis, synthesis, and evaluation. It's a fairly simple tool, but it still requires workers to use critical thinking to solve problems, and it does so without significant disruptions to their regular work. See Figures 9.2 and 9.3.

Problem Finding: Concern

Here are the four most common ways the C4 process is initiated within an organization:

1. *Alert response.* An individual employee reports a problem, and the TL or supervisor responds with a C4 card in hand.
2. *Individual response.* An individual employee experiences or observes a problem, grabs a C4 card, and initiates the process.
3. *Individual idea.* An individual has an idea about how to improve something in his or her work area, grabs a C4 card and initiates the process.
4. *Management response.* A manager or leader wants a team or an individual to address either a specific problem or goal in a business plan and provides a C4 card to begin the process.

Beyond the first few steps, all four ways follow the same process: identify the *concern*; find the *cause*; develop, evaluate, and implement

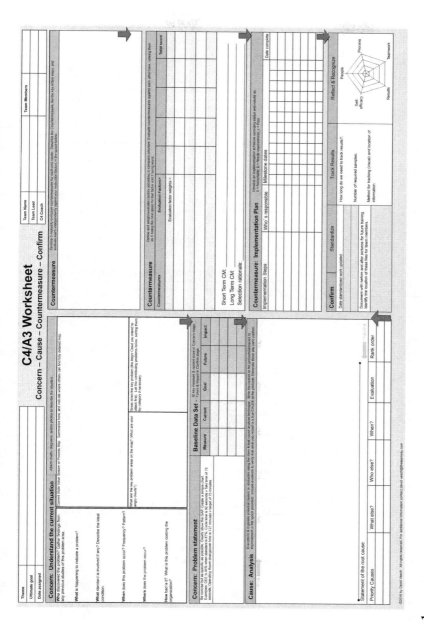

FIGURE 9.1

C4 A3 worksheet.

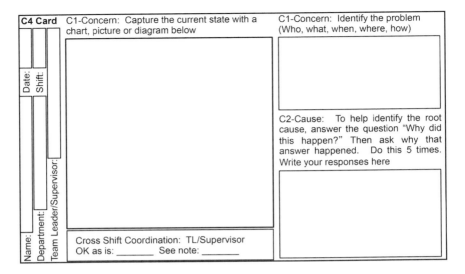

FIGURE 9.2
C4 card—front.

C3 - Evaluate your countermeasure						C3-Countermeasure: Capture the future state with a chart, picture or diagram below
Circle the appropriate ratings						
Ease	Easy	Medium	Hard			
Cost	$	$$	$$$	?		
Control	All	Some	Little	?		
Effective	Yes	Maybe	No			
Savings	$$$	$$	$	?		

Implementation Plan (what, who, and when):

Action steps	Who	When

C4-Confirm: Has the countermeasure been approved, implemented and standardized?

	No	Yes	Date	By whom	Reference #:
Approved:					
Implemented:					
Standardized:					

FIGURE 9.3
C4 card—back.

countermeasures; and *confirm* that countermeasures were effective and that the C4 process worked properly.

When using the C4 card, the critical success factor is the specific interaction between the individual and a coach working through the C4 process. Sometimes, of course, this interaction may result in the employee or supervisor deciding a chartered team would be more appropriate for the problem at hand. In such a case, a problem-solving effort that began with a C4 card would migrate to a C4 worksheet.

In the *alert response* scenario, all an individual employee has to do when they experience a problem is report it. This approach is most appropriate for problems that threaten production (i.e., if the problem isn't solved, people must stop working). Machine breakdowns (including computers in offices); errors made by operators; accidents or safety near misses; or missing parts, information, or tools are problems that could fall into this category. In organizations equipped with andon systems, systems designed to notify a succession of leaders in the case of a problem, the individual employee usually needs to activate the andon system manually (by pulling a cord or pressing a button).

When a team leader (TL) or supervisor arrives in response to an alert, the employee and TL/supervisor implement a short-term countermeasure together. They'll then grab a C4 card and document the problem; critically thinking through the *concern*, finding the root *cause*, and then developing and evaluating a long-term *countermeasure*. The most important element in this case is the response of the TL or supervisor. If the response is not immediate, the organization risks additional costs of delay in work or, even worse, losing track of the problem as the product, report, or activity continues without stopping. The C4 card serves to document the problem so that the organization can keep track of issues in the workplace, spot trends and follow-up on them to ensure a long-term *countermeasures* hold.

In the *individual response* scenario, when an employee experiences a problem he simply needs to grab a card (a supply of which should be kept near every workstation), fill in his name, and note what he thinks the problem is under C1: concern. In this category, the employee must identify the problem (who, what, when, where, and how). This process needs to be as simple as possible to encourage everyone to keep using the cards. Examples like: "Bottleneck for product flow in finishing," "Paper jam in network printer 3," or "No parts in the pick bin" are fine. At this point, no other details are required. This *individual response* approach is primarily useful for problems of minor annoyance. In organizations that have used C4 for some time, it may be appropriate for an individual employee to record other, more significant problems after activating the alert system, rather than simply waiting for a TL or supervisor to respond. This combination provides an immediate diagnosis of the problem that can help to speed the solution when a leader or supporting expert (maintenance tech, etc.) arrives to help.

The *individual idea* scenario uses the C4 card to capture employee ideas. An employee starts the card by filling in his or her name and a brief description of their idea in the C3-countermeasure section and then gives the card to the TL or supervisor at the earliest opportunity. Once an idea has been captured, the leader or C4 coach guides the employee through the process, helping to build skills in critical thinking, analysis, and evaluation.

Usually, these ideas are solutions to problems the employee has experienced in the past. The problem may not always be evident, so it's the solution that surfaces first. In other cases, an idea may relate to making something in the workplace work better, rather than addressing a specific problem. Ideas generated in this way are often powerful learning opportunities because individuals typically work much harder for the success of an idea they came up with. Of course, employees will only be willing to share their ideas if they feel safe doing so in the first place. This is why it's so important for companies to build relationships based on trust within the organization.

Most ideas generated by individual employees, like most ideas anywhere, will not be great, earth-shattering, big-money-saving game-changers. But even the worst of these ideas help to teach individuals how to analyze and evaluate ideas. It's much better if an individual concludes through his own analysis that his idea stinks, as opposed to having someone else (a boss, a parent, an expert, and a teacher) tell him it stinks.

The final scenario, *management response*, is often the best place to start. Almost every organization has a substantial list of valid, noncritical problems, and/or goals it has compiled over a long period of time. Using the C4 card to tackle items on this list allows the organization to roll out C4 in a controlled and deliberate manner. This approach is likely to make employees more receptive to the change than simply putting a bunch of cards about the workplace and telling people to fill them out as needed.

Though not a problem per se, a goal on a business plan is an expected level of performance. And the organization is not achieving the goal, or it wouldn't be in the plan. The C4 card and worksheet give managers real tools they can use to move toward their goals, rather than simply reviewing progress at a monthly meeting. To make the most effective use of these powerful tools, managers should routinely take a C4 card out into the work area and interact with employees to develop *countermeasures* that might take them to goal-level performance.

C4 Coaching

Regardless of how a C4 card is initiated, it's the interactive learning that occurs between an employee and a leader or C4 coach that makes it so powerful. Furthermore, making this process more visible to the workforce spreads the habit, encouraging others to report and think through workplace problems.

Regardless of how a leader secures a C4 card, his or her job is to teach individuals critical thinking and problem-solving skills. Immediately after a C4 card is initiated, the employee, the leader, or the C4 coach posts it on the C4 board. See Figure 9.4.

The reason for posting the C4 card is twofold: (1) it tells everyone in the area that a problem is being analyzed and (2) it keeps the problem visible, which helps to promote completion of the analysis.

For an *alert response*, the posting may take place after the leader and the employee have already applied a short-term countermeasure together. In the case of an *individual response* or *individual idea*, the leader may or may not have discussed the problem with the employee before posting the card. If it's a *management response*, the leader first discusses the problem with the employee and then posts the card to the board.

The board is organized so that cards can be tracked visually to completion. Cards are moved from column to column as related activities are in process or completed. The titles of the C4 board columns are named for the steps in setting C4 as a plastic explosive; mostly to make it interesting,

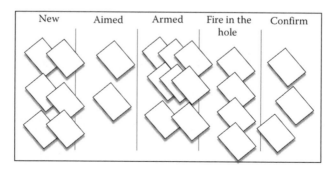

FIGURE 9.4
C4 board.

but also to keep titles short and simple. Each organization should feel free to create titles that work for them.

- "New" is where people will post their new problem reports or ideas
- "Aimed" means the coach has completed an initial discussion with the employee and the idea is waiting for input from other shifts or departments as needed
- "Armed" means the leader has reported the problem or idea to the department manager and received input from others, and that the coach and employee are evaluating *countermeasures*
- "Fire in the Hole" means the employee and coach have selected the best *countermeasure* and the implementation is in process.

The card moves from new to aimed after the leader or coach has completed an initial discussion with the employee. This discussion needs to occur on the same day the card is posted, as the employee continues working. The TL or supervisor serves as a coach to lead the employee through the C4 process, asking questions about the problem and the work environment, specifically giving the employee the opportunity to practice critical thinking and problem solving.

The supervisor may choose to assign the card, and the task of coaching the individual employee, to another employee who has been designated a C4 peer coach. These individuals have received a certain amount of training, allowing them to work with their peers in completing the C4 card.

The initial conversation should be friendly and focused on the employee. Even if the coach thinks the idea is the dumbest she's ever heard, she has to follow the process. People can learn skills related to analysis, synthesis, and evaluation from dumb ideas as well as good ones. Thus, it's important that the coach understands her role as one of teacher rather than judge.

The coach should seek to understand the *concern* by asking questions that make the employee think critically:

- Who discovered this problem?
- What happened, exactly?
- How often does it happen?
- Is there a pattern to when it happens (say every afternoon; or only on Wednesdays)?
- What did you do in the past when this problem occurred?
- Who else has to work around this issue?
- How bad is it?

If the identified problem is substantial, the peer coach needs to help the employee break it down into a solvable chunk or refer it to the department manager, so they can assemble a group or team to solve. Leaders should insist that coaches exert considerable effort to break down problems with employees, rather than simply refer them up the chain. A small piece of a large problem solved completely at the working level by an employee and his coach means the employee will be more willing to go through the process again. The cumulative effect of having many small problems solved is also likely to outweigh the effect of solving a single large problem over a longer period of time.

As the coach secures answers to the questions listed above, thus helping the individual more clearly define the problem, he or she writes the answers on the C4 card in the appropriate space.

Cause

Next, the coach leads the employee through a "5 whys" analysis to get to the root *cause*. This activity may require more challenging questions to help the individual think through the causes thoroughly. A note of caution: it's very easy to fall into the trap of identifying solutions as causes. Whenever an answer reflects the absence of something (e.g., "no training" or "no standardized work" or "lack of time," etc.), it's important that the coach have the employee identify the underlying problem he or she thinks the answer should solve.

Another trap easily fallen into during analysis is blaming, with the most frequently blamed entity being management. Often, individuals and groups try to work through why something has happened but get sidetracked by citing a policy or inattentive leader as the root *cause*. While a company policy or manager may contribute to a problem in the work environment, leaders need to coach employees to focus on causes upon which they can take specific action. If the answers to the five whys take the problem solver outside his area of control, the leader should coach him or her to refocus on a path that will lead to a cause they can affect personally.

Countermeasures

Many companies have created simple forms to capture employee ideas or document problems, but few of these approaches require the submitter to analyze and evaluate his own ideas or *countermeasures*. However, to drive learning and cognitive development to the highest levels, organizations need to teach this critical skill. Like the C4 worksheet, the C4 card requires that the employee and their coach think through key elements of the proposed *countermeasure*, evaluating its *cost, ease to do, control* and *effectiveness*, as well as the savings likely to be achieved by implementing the proposed solution.

Often, an employee will need to interact with support staff to get enough information for a proper evaluation. For example, he may have to get technical estimates from engineering, financial information from accounting, or materials costs from purchasing. Because the C4 process requires the employee to round up this information—with the help of the coach—the effort will require specific scheduling to ensure that the employee's normal work still gets done. The organization may have to insist that support people schedule meeting times with the employee at *his* workplace rather than their own. Such a shift in focus clearly emphasizes the priority a company places on developing a problem-solving and "go and see" culture.

If an evaluated *countermeasure* turns out to be a good one, the employee and coach plan its implementation, obtain approvals or complete work orders for maintenance or engineering support, schedule the implementation, and execute the schedule.

All of this may sound like a rather time-consuming process, but in the majority of cases, everyone is able to get through the entire process, including implementing the solution, in a single day. Imagine the impact of such execution-focused activity. Employees get positive attention and assistance when they report problems or share ideas. As more people see ideas and solutions impact their workplaces, they become more likely to report their own problems and share their own ideas. Of course, this scenario is a two-edged sword. On the one hand, the organization has a vibrant, engaged, and excited workforce sharing hundreds of problems and ideas every day. On the other, however, the company has to make sure that only the best of these ideas get rapidly implemented.

The question then is, "Where do we get the resources to implement all these solutions?" The answer is simple—they are there already, working every day: employees, TLs, and supervisors throughout the company provide the resources. The organization has to equip them with the skills they need, then empower them to make decisions, approve action plans, and obtain materials and support so that they can take all the steps required to solve problems effectively. Expectations of leaders must change to require that their first priority, the most important aspect of their job, is to teach.

The communication of problems or ideas that need higher-level support must also be fast and focused. Organizations with lean meeting structures are already positioned to include very brief problem reviews in their daily operation. C4 boards aid in this communication. As leaders make daily trips through the workplace, they'll be able to see and review the status of all C4 cards in progress.

Confirm

To wrap up the process, the completed card moves to the *confirm* column on the C4 board and the coach leads the employee through reflection on the process, asking her to answer specific questions about the way she approached the *concern*, *cause*, and *countermeasure* stages, and then following up on the implemented solutions to ensure they were as effective as estimated.

Completed cards are kept on file, with their contents entered into a database so that both the problem and the solution are available for future reference to everyone in the organization. There are a variety of ways to capture this information, but resist the temptation to automate this entire process. The visual nature of the C4 process ensures that everyone knows the expectations and sees the status of ideas. Perhaps, a designated individual could walk through the workplace and collect the completed cards from the *confirm* columns on all the C4 boards, then enter them into the database before filing them.

A FEW THINGS I'VE LEARNED SINCE THE C4 BOOK WAS PUBLISHED

I am awed and amazed by how much people teach me while I'm teaching them. In working with companies and individuals using the C4 process, I have discovered new ways to present things and new ways to encourage people. I've learned that sometimes people just need a list to follow before they try something.

Working the C4 Card

1. Post the card. Regardless of where the action began, the card needs a problem/idea along with a name, and it needs to get stuck on the board.

2. The leader responsible for that board (which should be integrated into a team information board as described in Chapter 7 of this book) pulls the card when he or she has time set aside in their standardized work to do so.

3. After a quick review, the leader assigns a coach, often assigning himself/herself to the job. Another excellent option though is a peer coach. Recruit people who have submitted cards in the past to help others through the process.

4. Dialogue. This is the most important function we perform. This dialogue teaches those critical thinking skills. The C4 coach deliberately asks who, what, when, where, and how questions to the person who submitted the card in a friendly and open discussion. Then, the questions turn to whys, as we talk through potential root causes and decide what else needs to be done. After this initial discussion, the coach takes the submitter through the initial evaluation, a simple review of the scope of the problem. It identifies the effort that it may take to solve the problem along with the potential impact solving the problem is likely to have. This evaluation determines whether they need to keep working on the problem, drop it, or escalate it. See Figure 9.5.

5. Cross-unit coordination. If in the dialogue they decide to keep working on the problem or idea, the coach will post its card in the next column to the right on the C4 board, to indicate that anyone else who wants to comment on the problem or idea should do so. In workplaces with multiple shifts, this gives others a chance to comment before a solution surprises them. The card may also need to be

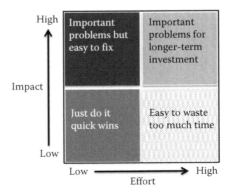

FIGURE 9.5
Initial evaluation.

shared across team or department boundaries, which occurs when the coach/TL goes to the supervisors meeting to share the new problem or idea.

6. Adjust the details. After others have had a chance to comment, the coach and submitter refine the problem and the cause in further discussion, sometimes clarifying the next steps and sometimes concluding that the problem or idea should not go further.

7. Develop countermeasures. Up to this point, we have focused on clearly defining the problem and finding its causes. During this, it is very likely that many ideas will have surfaced as solutions. The coach has to prevent acting on any of these solutions or countermeasures until the submitter has had a chance to consider them and come up with his or her own remedies. Coaches ensure that multiple countermeasures are developed and considered, rather than just running with the first thing that comes up. Coaches also require and assist the submitters in evaluating the different options to decide which to take. Together, they will plan how to execute the countermeasure, and set a timeline for the execution of the countermeasure. The timeline might be a simple "Just do it" executed immediately, or it may take more complex coordination to schedule.

8. Confirm. After all of this, the coach leads the submitter through a directed reflection activity to review what was learned as a result of this action. They move the card to the *complete* column on the C4 board where someone (perhaps an administrative assistant) will routinely collect all completed cards from all the boards and either catalog them in a file, or digitize them for a knowledge management system.

Make It Your Own

Something that I encourage organizations to do is to take the C4 board and cards and make them their own. There are many variants of these kinds of idea boards, but most include a column for new ideas, one for those in process, and one for those that are done. Most people change the names of the columns from aimed, armed, and fire in the hole to concern, cause, countermeasure, and confirm. See Figure 9.6. Some also present a method of showing those cards that get escalated to higher levels because they may take significant resources to implement, or because they affect a larger part of the organization. See Figure 9.7.

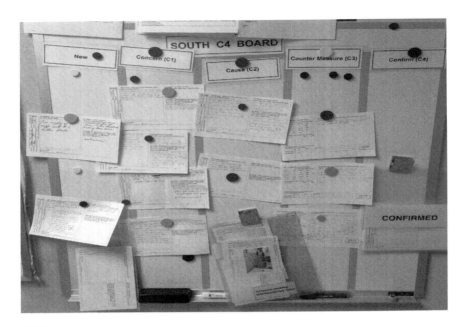

FIGURE 9.6
C4 board.

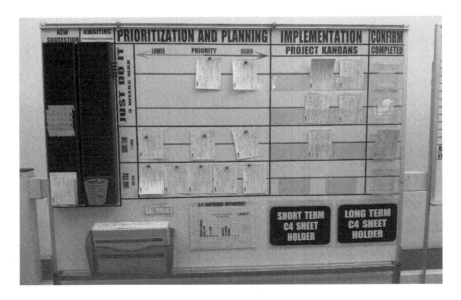

FIGURE 9.7
C4 board.

SOME RANDOM IDEAS ABOUT RIGOROUS PROBLEM SOLVING

Farming, Not Mining

Earlier in this chapter, I mentioned how most suggestion systems are oriented toward idea mining. The underlying thought is that the ideas are in there somewhere and we have to dig them out. What we really need to be doing is idea farming. Most ideas burst forth and die quickly because they aren't suitable solutions to problems in the workplace. All of them however, are suited to inspire learning.

If we view our work system as a mine, the implication is that everything we need to succeed is contained within and we have to dig it out until there's no more. It's hard on people because we're always digging deeper and harder. To get the things we need, we often have to remove more material than what we're mining for and often discard the extra stuff.

If we instead view our work system as a farm, we realize that everything we do has to be sustainable for the long haul. The system requires employee engagement, and the C4 system is a tool to achieve that engagement. The work that people do, and their experiences with good, problem-free days as well as bad, problem-filled days serves as the weather and climate. People are the soil from which ideas grow. Those ideas are like seeds that need to be planted and nurtured as they grow into more effective solutions. Sometimes the ideas will be weeds, sometimes they'll be flowers, and sometimes they will bear fruit.

We can look at data the same way. "Data mining" is a popular phrase for businesses these days, and it seems "Big Data" is like a big coal mine that we're going to go digging around in. For an effective workplace, we need to define the data we need. Often, we aren't collecting the right data to make the right decisions. Most of the time, we'll have to make adjustments to what data we collect and how. Data are a farm. We have to plant and grow, rotate crops and fertilize them, and sometimes spray to kill what's there before we can plant new and different crops. We'll get weeds that need to be pulled (bad data that misleads us), but when we have a harvest (data that leads to successful solutions), we'll have cause to celebrate.

Directed Reflection

We can turn any event or activity into a learning focused event or activity simply by studying what happened after the fact. This is not new.

Plan–do–check–act tells us that we have to check things after they've been done and it's been around since the 1930s. While I was in the US Army stationed at Fort Knox, Training and Doctrine Command (TRADOC) used my unit to develop procedures for more effective after action reviews (AAR), so military forces could systematically review everything that happened during a given mission and learn from it. The most effective training we ever did was called a situational training exercise (STX) that may have been based on some kind of drill, such as breaching a mine-field, or conducting a raid. We would run the scenario, have an AAR, then immediately run the scenario again to be followed by another AAR. As the learning cycles went faster, our performance improved. If we want to get better at something like problem solving (or even just the way we do our work), we have to hold a review session afterwards to see what we were supposed to do (the plan) versus what we actually did and how it turned out. We should always end these sessions with a focus on what we need to do differently in the next cycle to improve performance.

Software development runs in iterations. Each iteration should be followed by a focused retrospective. I have been told way too many times how time pressure from senior leaders prevents people from doing better retrospectives (retros). In problem solving for workplaces, I've run into the same things, so I added the deliberate review and reflect section to the C4 worksheet in the bottom right corner. After the team has solved the problem (or implemented the solution, whether or not it solved the problem!), they need to review what they did.

Several organizations do this reflection piece very well for the most part. What we're doing with students in the Master of Business Operational Excellence (MBOE) program at the Ohio State University is to begin every morning with a review of the previous day's or previous week's course material or activities, focusing on the key lessons learned. We also ask students to focus on how they could apply those lessons in their own workplaces, and where they think the gaps in their learning are, so that we can identify ways to close those gaps. Students first review their own notes and identify their private learning, then share in a small group as one of the team members records the team input on a flip chart. Following this, we give every team the opportunity to share their discoveries. The entire process wraps up after 30 minutes and sets the focus for the day.

At the end of every day (the MBOE meets eight times over the course of a year for 4.5 days of focused learning each time), we close the day with a quick Plus/Delta review of the day. This highlights both what students enjoyed and what their key lessons learned were (the Plus), and gives them an opportunity to provide feedback about what they did not think was particularly helpful (the Delta). These end-of-the-day sessions are typically very quick and unstructured, but we also ask students to write for 1 minute, focusing on how they could apply the lessons of the day in their workplace.

For projects, problem-solving teams, quality circles, learning circles, kaizen events, etc., leaders need to demand this kind of reflection to reinforce learning and improvement. One of these review activities I have seen asks people to answer the following questions:

- Insight: what were the key lessons we learned today?
- How has today made us more respectful to people?
- What challenges exist to applying what we learned today?
- What actions are required to implement and sustain what we learned today?

Remember to focus on what we specifically need to do differently next time, and then make sure that the next time is very soon.

CHAPTER SUMMARY

Remove your suggestion box to make ideas and reported problems more transparent in the workplace. Making them visible allows everyone to know whether or not we're making progress on them.

The C4 process focuses on learning and speeding up learning cycles. It is highly structured to ensure that the problem-solving process is followed thoroughly with rigor in order to build key skills like critical thinking, quantitative analysis, creativity, planning and organizing, executing, and evaluating. It further teaches leaders how to have a focused conversation or dialogue with their people to build more trusting relationships in the workplace.

Everyone should personalize the C4 worksheet, card, and board to work for their own workplace, so that people will take more ownership and pride in seeing them through. We will make the worksheet and card available to readers in editable form through our website at www.leadersights.com and www.thec4process.com.

Consider your workplace more like a farm that needs to be nurtured than a mine that needs to be exploited. This applies to data and to ideas, but impact people the most.

Always stop and take the time to reflect after any activity involving a team of people. Have them focus on what lessons they learned and discuss how what they did deviated from their plan or their expectations. This is critical for creating a learning organization.

10

Epilogue

Love. Learn. Let go. Everything I've written ties back to these three simple/ complex behaviors. I hope that many of the dots I have shared through the previous chapters have connected into a picture of what you can do to get yourself and your workplace ready for the future.

We started with a framework that has as its foundation an idea I called dynamic stability. Three metaphors capture this idea:

- The living human body, which on the outside stops growing upwardly in our late teens, with our skeletal system to hold things erect and stable while the unending hum of all the other bio-systems keeps everything dynamic.
- An aircraft carrier at sea with its rigid flat-topped structure and enormous size, these ships are not designed to be nimble, so on the sea it looks as stable as an island, but below decks, 5000 sailors circulate like blood cells in veins to keep the ship running. Then, in response to opportunities or threats, the air wing deploys its supersonic jets in any direction to explore, protect, attack, or assist, a completely dynamic capability.
- An expert whitewater kayaker, where the rushing river is always changing the dynamics of its interaction with the boat. The kayaker, using thousands of adjustments every second, presents the outward picture of stability, staying upright, and purposefully navigating through the torrent to a visionary destination.

It is all a balancing act. If we lock down too much stability, we'll be unable to respond quickly enough to changing conditions or requirements. If we're constantly changing and reinventing and refocusing, we never get good enough to keep customers coming back or to keep people working for us and with us.

I've tried to emphasize making rigid structures in the workplace that provide the stability we need to improve, but having defined ways (more rigid structures) of making changes to any of those structures very quickly. Stability is in the hands of leaders who design and build those rigid but still changeable systems. Change, despite so many calls for leaders to drive change, really should be in the hands of the workforce.

The workforce has to be engaged, but it won't be without structures that guide our behavior. We worked through four cultural stages within which a workplace may find itself: compliance, involvement, enthusiasm, and engagement. We didn't really talk about how fragile each can be, and how easy it is for a new leader to collapse an engaged culture all the way back to compliance with a single stupid decision, just like a failure in the foundation can bring a giant skyscraper to the ground.

Satisfaction plays a huge role in building the culture, and throughout the book I tried to show how the tools we use to get things done can push satisfaction up or down, but the common denominator is trust between people in the workplace. Leaders have to build trust. I tied that in to the core of the four zones of the integral leadership model.

If we acknowledge that the workforce should drive changes in the workplace, then the real secret is what enables and empowers the workforce to engage and act with self-determination. I believe it is self-efficacy. I spent a lot of time defining the outcomes of high self-efficacy: willingness to change the workspace, to try new things, and to persist through failures, and defining the contributors to the same: mastery experiences, a supportive and visual learning environment, performance feedback from a trusted partner and work system, and true control over the workspace assigned.

Everything I've described came with some application of a tool, structure, or system. In the description of the continuous improvement engine, I tried to capture how these all fit together to create a great and satisfying workplace.

What I really want leaders to do, though, is just create flow. Whether it's the flow of information, or materials, or people in getting work done, it all needs to flow smoothly with no delays. But that's just the physical piece of flow. The real deal is psychological flow, the feeling of being caught up in the moment, where time stands still and effort feeds exhilaration. You know what I mean…being in "the zone."

By applying the principles and techniques in this book, you can create the kind of workplace people love; one where they can't wait to get started and where leaders have to go and tell everyone when it's time to leave; one where people enter and stay in "the zone." This state of flow comes largely through the same channels as self-efficacy, particularly mastery and control. But two other key factors are in play as well: immediate performance feedback, which can only come from the work itself, and clearly defined rules, which in our case means standardized work and challenging goals.

THE VLO

More importantly, by applying the principles and techniques and maybe some of the ideas I've shared, you'll create the foundation for a Vigorous Learning Organization (VLO). This structure gives us the best chance for a survivable and sustainable long-term future. As Robert "Doc" Hall initially described in his book *Compression: Meeting the Challenges of Sustainability through Vigorous Learning Enterprises,* the VLO has as its core a common mission with a meaningful purpose. Interacting through the mission are key principles of Leadership and "Seeing the whole."

I have had the good fortune of working closely with Doc and others over the past several years in the Compression Institute. Our dialog and discussions shaped much of what has appeared in this book. We started discussing servant leadership but agreed there had to be more. Integral leadership from Chapter 6 is what I think the "more" is.

Doc refers to "Seeing the whole" as "Compression Thinking" and over the years since the book was published, he has written extensively and created dozens of illustrations of this. You can find all of them at www.compression.org.

Also interacting through the common mission is the primary structural component, the rigorous learning system. This system is built on the scientific method. It is a further refinement of the system I have described in Chapter 9. The outcomes of the rigorous learning system and systems thinking are collected under "Behavior for learning." These behaviors roughly parallel those I described in Chapters 3, 6, and 8 for leaders. I'm bringing this into the discussion of this book because while I have sort of described taking one step into the future from lean management toward vigorous learning, Doc has thought through hundreds of variants of the future for the long term that stretch the concepts and the imagination. See Figure 10.1.

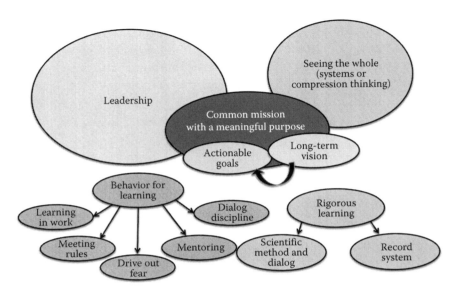

FIGURE 10.1
Vigorous learning organization.

Leading this transformation, this first step, will still be very difficult for you as a leader. You will have people who won't respond to anything you do or offer. You will have others who push your limits by trying to go too far and too fast. You'll have people who will hate you no matter what you do. But you'll also have those who love you. Roll with it.

To send you off, I've created this permanent to do list for you. This isn't earth-shattering, but put this list where you can see it every day or every time you're about to bust a vein.

PERMANENT TO-DO LIST

- Share your vision. Make sure people know where you want to go. Tell a compelling story and be passionate about it. If your vision doesn't inspire passion, redo it!
- Be the model. Whatever you do as a leader you know people are watching. They will do what you do, so do what's right.
- Build relationships. You can only do that by interacting with people, so go and see, ask questions, and show respect. Make yours a great place to work.

- Carefully develop leaders. Everyone is potentially a leader. Start with those who believe things can be better, then build their skills, challenge them with important goals, and get out of the way (love, learn, let go.)
- Build teams. No one can do this alone. Build teams around the work you do and around problems you encounter. Keep teams small so they can build great relationships too.
- Be a continuous learner. Understand the work that everyone does. Go, see, and learn. Listen. Find problems and help people think them through. Develop creative solutions with them.
- Pay attention to metrics. Be careful to watch what you measure. If you aren't getting the behaviors you want, you're probably measuring the wrong things. Fix that.
- Stay positive. You will have setbacks. But don't ever be the jerk that sucks all the energy out of a room with overwhelming negativity. You are creating a bright future for your workplace. Hold that in your mind to help keep you positive.
- Do it all again tomorrow, only a little better.

Love. Learn. Let go. That's leadership. Good luck!

Bibliography

Bandura, A. 1982. Self-efficacy mechanism in human agency. *American Psychologist*, 37, 122–147.

Bandura, A. 1991. Social cognitive theory of self-regulation. *Organizational Behavior and Human Decision Processes*, 50, 248–287.

Banham, R. 2002. *The Ford Century: Ford Motor Company and the Innovations that Shaped the World*. New York: Artisan.

Benson, J. and DeMaria Barry, T. 2011. *Personal Kanban: Mapping Work, Navigating Life*. Seattle: CreateSpace Independent Publishing Platform.

Bloom, B. S. et al. 1956. *Taxonomy of Educational Objectives: Handbook I: Cognitive Domain*. New York: David McKay.

Collins, J. 2001. *Good to Great: Why Some Companies Make the Leap and Others Don't*. New York: HarperCollins.

Collins, J. and Hansen, M. T. 2011. *Great by Choice: Uncertainty, Chaos, and Luck—Why Some Thrive Despite Them All*. New York: HarperCollins.

Csikszentmihalyi, M. 1990. *Flow: The Psychology of Optimal Experience*. New York: Harper & Row.

Deutschman, A. 2007. *Change or Die: The Three Keys to Change at Work and in Life*. New York: Harper Business.

Duhigg, C. 2014. *The Power of Habit: Why We Do What We Do in Life and Business*. New York: Random House.

Foner, E. and Garraty, J. (eds). 1991. *The Reader's Companion to American History*. New York: Houghton-Mifflin Co. Inc.

Ford, H. 1926. *Today and Tomorrow*. New York: Doubleday Page; Reprint 1988 Productivity Press.

Gist, M. E. and Mitchell, T. R. 1992. Self-efficacy: A theoretical analysis of its determinants and malleability. *Academy of Management Review*, 17, 183–211.

Green, T. B. and Hayes, M. 2003. *The Belief System: The Secret to Motivation and Improved Performance*. Winston-Salem, North Carolina: The Hayes Group International, Inc.

Hall, R. W. 2009. *Compression: Meeting the Challenges of Sustainability through Vigorous Learning Enterprises*. New York: Productivity Press.

Harrow, A. 1972. *A Taxonomy of Psychomotor Domain: A Guide for Developing Behavioral Objectives*. New York: David McKay.

Herzberg, F. 1987. One more time: How do you motivate employees? *Harvard Business Review Special Reprint 87507*, September–October, 6–16.

Hock, D. 1995. The chaordic organization: Out of control and into order. *World Business Academy Perspectives*, 9(1), 5–18.

Hunter, J. 1998. *The Servant: A Simple Story about the True Essence of Leadership*. Roseville, California: Prima Publishing.

Hunter, J. C. 2004. *The World's Most Powerful Leadership Principle: How to Be a Servant Leader*. New York: Crown.

Juran, J. 1967. The QC circle phenomenon. *Industrial Quality Control*, January, pp. 25–34.

Kouzes, J. M. and Posner, B. Z. 2002. *The Leadership Challenge*, 3rd edn. San Francisco, California: Jossey-Bass.

Kramer, R. M. 1996. Divergent realities and convergent disappointments in the hierarchic relation: Trust and the intuitive auditor at work. In *Trust in Organizations: Frontiers of Theory and Research*, R. M. Kramer and T. R. Tyler (eds), 216–245, Thousand Oaks, California: Sage Publications.

Krathwohl, D. R., Bloom, B. S., and Masia, B. B. 1964. *Taxonomy of Educational Objectives: Handbook II: Affective Domain*. New York: David McKay.

Lareau, W. 2002. *Office Kaizen: Transforming Office Operations into a Strategic Competitive Advantage*. Milwaukee, Wisconsin: ASQ Quality Press.

Larson, C. E. and LaFasto, F. M. J. 1989. *Teamwork: What Must Go Right/What Can Go Wrong*. Newbury Park, California: Sage.

Maslow, A. H. 1943. A theory of human motivation. *Psychological Review*, 50(4), 370.

Ohno, T. 1988. *Workplace Management*. Portland, Oregon: Productivity Press.

Pfeffer, J. 2010. *Power: Why Some People Have It and Others Don't*. New York: HarperCollins.

Pfeffer, J. 2015. *Leadership BS: Fixing Workplaces and Careers One Truth at a Time*. New York: HarperCollins.

Ryan, R. M. and Deci, E. L. 2000. Self-determination theory and the facilitation of intrinsic motivation, social development, and well-being. *American Psychologist*, 55(1), 68–78.

Stajkovic, A. D. and Luthans, F. 1998. Social cognitive theory and self-efficacy: Going beyond traditional motivational and behavioral approaches. *Organizational Dynamics*, Spring, 62–73.

Toyoda, E. 1987. *Toyota: Fifty Years in Motion*. New York: Harper & Row.

Tuckman, B. 1965. Developmental sequence in small groups. *Psychological Bulletin*, 63(6), 384–399.

Tuckman, B. W. and Jensen, M. 1977. Stages of small-group development revisited. *Group & Organization Studies*, 2, 419–427.

Veech, D. S. 2004a. A person-centered approach to sustaining a lean environment—Job design for self-efficacy. *Defense Acquisition Review Journal*, September–October, 158–171.

Veech, D. S. 2004b. Flexibility through stability—Enhancing behaviors. *Cost Management*, September–October, 15–22.

Veech, D. S. and Damodaraswamy, P. 2011. *The C4 Process: Four Critical Steps to Better Work*. Lexington, Kentucky: Robert G Clark Consulting LLC.

Wilbur, K. 2000. *Integral Psychology: Consciousness, Spirit, Psychology, Therapy*. Boston, Massachusetts: Shambhala.

Yingling, J. and Damodaraswamy, P. 2011. *Creating and Sustaining Highly Effective Lean Standardized Work Systems*. Lexington, Kentucky: Robert G Clark Consulting LLC.

Index